THE LORD'S SUPPER
IN THE NEW TESTAMENT

STUDIES IN BIBLICAL THEOLOGY

THE LORD'S SUPPER IN THE NEW TESTAMENT

A. J. B. HIGGINS

SCM PRESS LTD
56 BLOOMSBURY STREET
LONDON

First published May 1952
Reprinted December 1954
Reprinted February 1956

Printed in Great Britain by
Robert Cunningham and Sons Ltd.
Longbank Works, Alva

CONTENTS

		PAGE
	FOREWORD	7
I	THE LAST SUPPER AND THE MINISTRY OF JESUS	9
II	THE NATURE OF THE LAST SUPPER	13
III	THE EUCHARISTIC SAYINGS OF JESUS: THEIR FORM	24
IV	THE EUCHARISTIC SAYINGS OF JESUS: THEIR MEANING	45
V	TWO TYPES OF EUCHARIST?	56
VI	PAUL'S TEACHING ON THE LORD'S SUPPER	64
VII	JOHANNINE EUCHARISTIC DOCTRINE	74
	CONCLUSION	89
	Index of References	90
	Index of Authors	95

FOREWORD

DESPITE the bewildering wealth of the literature on the Lord's Supper in the New Testament there is room for a fresh monograph in English, for continental scholars have been more productive in this field of recent years than English-speaking writers. I have therefore thought it useful to take account of the best work on the subject in the writing of this book. But this study is the fruit of a fresh and independent investigation of a fascinating problem, or rather, of a whole series of problems. In some cases the result has been the abandonment of views formerly held, notably as regards the nature of the Last Supper; and here I acknowledge my deep indebtedness to the work of J. Jeremias (*Die Abendmahlsworte Jesu*, 2nd edn., 1949), who brings to bear all the weight of his knowledge of the Hebrew and Aramaic sources.

For one who welcomes the new emphasis on eucharistic worship in a section of his own communion, as well as in others, it would have been tempting to emerge at the conclusion from the study and to mount the ecclesiastical platform. But the purpose of this book is to try and shed fresh light on the teaching of the New Testament itself—a task sufficiently exacting.

CHAPTER ONE

THE LAST SUPPER AND THE MINISTRY OF JESUS

THE Christian sacrament of the Eucharist, called in different branches of the Church by a variety of names (Holy Communion, the Lord's Supper, the Mass) and celebrated and understood in widely different ways, is the direct descendant of the Last Supper of Jesus with his disciples. The cleavage of opinion as to whether Jesus did or did not 'found' the Church, has its counterpart in the debate on the origin of the Eucharist. Was it deliberately 'instituted' by Jesus himself, or is it a natural and perhaps inevitable development which began in the earliest days of the Church, but which Jesus had neither foreseen nor intended? These two questions of the Church and the Eucharist are inseparably connected, just as it is impossible to isolate Israel and the Passover from one another. The Church is the successor of Israel as the people of God, and its Eucharist is the successor of the Passover. The answer to the question, Did Jesus found the Church and institute the Eucharist? cannot be a simple yes or no, but lies somewhere between. He gathered together a small band of followers whom he intended to be the nucleus of a new religious community; this has developed into the Church as we know it. He gave instructions at his last meal with the twelve that in the relatively short time between his parting from them and his reunion with them in the Kingdom of God, the annual Passover was to be observed by them and by the community as it grew in memory of the greater deliverance than that from Egypt wrought through *him*: this has developed into the Eucharist in all its variety of forms.

After the arrest of John the Baptist Jesus began his preaching in Galilee. 'The time is fulfilled, and the Kingdom of God is at hand; repent, and believe in the good news' (Mark 1.15). John also had proclaimed the imminence of some great happening, but what he expected was the wrath to come (Luke 3.7; Matt. 3.7), and the 'mightier one', the Messiah, was to bring not a baptism of water like his, but a baptism of fire (Luke 3.16; Matt. 3.11). The only way of escape from judgment was repentance backed up by good works, and baptism at his hands as a pledge of repentance. Jesus came to John's baptism not on his own account but as a representative of his people, whose repentance was symbolized in his baptism. That he had his own nation of Israel primarily in mind during his ministry is manifest, and his choice of twelve chief disciples from among his followers expresses his belief that a new Israel would replace the old. His preaching and theirs was to actualize the national repentance symbolically represented in his baptism by proclaiming the good news that the Kingdom, the rule of God was already active in his works and in their works performed in his name.[1] In other words, the mission of Jesus was to bring men to obedience to God and to submission to his sovereign rule, to make *de facto* among men the Kingdom of God which was his *de iure*.

There are, however, other sayings of Jesus which show that he cherished eschatological hopes of a final *dénouement*. Attempts have been made to get rid of them, but they represent an essential aspect of his thought. And their significant feature, shared with Jesus' prophecies of his suffering, is that they concern the Son of Man. This title Jesus derived from Dan. 7, where Israel, under the corporate figure of 'one like a son of man', receives a kingdom to replace the evil world dominions, and he used it, in conjunction with the concept of the Suffering Servant in Deutero-Isaiah, in a Messianic sense (Mark 8.29, 31). Therefore, while it is true that Jesus does not relate the coming of the Son of Man to the coming or the presence of the Kingdom of God in so many words, it is difficult to see how he could possibly have kept the two separate, since the theme of his preaching was the Kingdom of God, and

---

[1] Luke 11.20; Matt. 12.28; Luke 10.9, 11; Matt. 10.7.

The Last Supper and the Ministry of Jesus

the notion of kingdom is central to Dan. 7. It seems, indeed, that Jesus chose the self-designation Son of Man precisely because of the association of the two ideas. Similarly, we do not find and we do not need an explicit declaration: 'I am the Servant of God', in order to be persuaded that he regarded himself as the fulfilment of Deutero-Isaiah's ideal. This is not the place to discuss the matter further. Suffice it to say that Jesus, in some way unknown to us, and perhaps not clear to him, expected the consummation of the Kingdom in all its power to take place quite soon, that he associated this consummation with his coming in glory as the Son of Man (the Parousia), and that this belief was mistaken.[1]

As Vincent Taylor says, 'the thought of the Kingdom, so central in the Galilaean teaching, glows in the very shadow of the Cross. Jesus both lives and dies absorbed in the thought of the Reign of God.'[2] The Last Supper was a farewell meal, but at the same time an anticipation of the Messianic banquet. Not until the fulfilment of the Kingdom of God would Jesus again eat the Passover and drink the fruit of the vine (Luke 22.16, 18; Mark 14.25). 'From the time of Isaiah onward, it had been recognized by the prophets that the true Israel of God is the faithful remnant of an apostate people.'[3] The twelve, as the nucleus of a new Israel, are promised the privilege of a share in the Kingdom (Luke 22.29 f). When did the Church begin? It blossomed forth under the dazzling light of the resurrection experience. But the seed had already been sown. The twelve disciples, chosen to continue the proclamation of the Kingdom, were the closest intimates of Jesus. They were a remnant of old Israel, and the nucleus of a new people of God, the 'little flock' to whom God will give the joys of the Kingdom (Luke 12.32, a clear echo of Dan. 7.27), and who will share the responsibilities by sitting on thrones judging the twelve tribes of (new) Israel (Luke 22.30; Matt. 19.28). If we

---

[1] For this point of view cf. T. W. Manson, *The Teaching of Jesus*, 2nd edn., 1935, pp. 136, 278, 282. Cf. Mark 8.38; 9.1; 13.26; 14.62.
[2] *Jesus and His Sacrifice*, 1943 (=1937), p. 259.
[3] C. H. Dodd, *History and the Gospel*, 1938, p. 136, who cites Isa. 4.3-5; Mal. 3.16 f.; 4.1 f.

may trust Luke here, Jesus at the Last Supper confirmed to his disciples what was already clear to them, that they were no longer free to go their own ways, but voluntarily bound one to the other and to him both now and in the future in what Paul was to call the 'body of Christ'.

As the Son of Man and the Kingdom are inseparable, so the Messiah must have his own Messianic community. 'For the Son of Man in Daniel is not a mere individual: he is the representative of "the people of the saints of the Most High" and has set himself the task of making this people of God, the ἐκκλησία, a reality.'[1] 'From this point of view', K. L. Schmidt goes on, 'the so-called institution of the Lord's Supper can be shown to be the *formal* founding of the Church.' The italics are mine, for the twelve had already been chosen as the beginning of the new community. Now, on the eve of parting from them, Jesus confirms his choice and binds them to unbroken allegiance to him in his absence until the *Parousia* by the command to observe the Passover henceforth in remembrance of the salvation wrought through *him*. They may thus, as Schmidt suggests, have been regarded by Jesus as a sort of sect or synagogue within Judaism.[2] They were to be like their fellow Jews in observing the Passover, but different from them in that henceforth 'between the times' their thoughts at that ancient festival were to be set on a greater deliverance than that from Egypt, because they were the embodiment of true Israel and a remnant in the midst of an Israel which had crowned its killing of the prophets and messengers of God by rejecting and slaying the Messiah himself.

---

[1] K. L. Schmidt, *The Church*, 1950, p. 40, translated by J. R. Coates from G. Kittel, *Theologisches Wörterbuch zum Neuen Testament*. See also in n. 1 references to other statements of this truth, especially that of G. Gloege, *Reich Gottes und Kirche im Neuen Testament*, 1929, pp. 218, 228: 'The saviour is only saviour as the creator of a new, redeemed and justified people; ... the Χριστός can no more be Christ without the ἐκκλησία than the ποιμήν can be shepherd without the ποίμνιον.' In Matt. 16.16-18 this is very clear. The acceptance by Jesus of the dignity of Messiah in the confession of Peter is followed by the Messiah's declaration of his intention to create his own *ecclesia*.

[2] Op. cit., pp. 48-50. Schmidt finds a certain analogy in the sect of reforming priests at Damascus known to us in the so-called 'Zadokite Work'.

CHAPTER TWO

THE NATURE OF THE LAST SUPPER

It will have been gathered from the preceding chapter that in this book the Last Supper of Jesus with his disciples is held to have been a Passover meal. The difficulties of coming to a decision are strikingly revealed in the sharp divergence of opinion among scholars on the matter. Strong arguments can be advanced on both sides, and it is unlikely that complete agreement will ever be reached. This is not a purely academic question, of interest only to scholars, for upon our answer depend our interpretation of the sayings of Jesus at his last meal with his friends, and our understanding of the Eucharist. A recent writer, while deciding that the Last Supper was a Passover meal, does not think that the paschal interpretation of it depends on this fact, because paschal ideas were bound to have been present in the minds of the gathering in the upper room in any case owing to the proximity of the Passover feast.[1] But the question of the nature of the Last Supper is of greater importance than this. It does not seem justifiable to attach paschal significance to the meal unless there are strong grounds for the belief that it was an actual celebration of the Passover. Attempts have been made to settle the question with the help of astronomy, but the results are indecisive. In the most likely year, A.D. 30, the balance of probability falls on Nisan 15th as the day of the crucifixion, but this is not certain. We must therefore fall back on the New Testament narratives themselves.

The clash of views about the character of the Last Supper is due to the disagreement of the Synoptic Gospels and the Fourth Gospel, and to alleged difficulties in the Synoptic representation of the Last Supper as a Passover meal. According to the Synoptic Gospels, the Last Supper took place on the evening of Thursday,

[1] F. J. Leenhardt, *Le sacrement de la sainte cène*, 1948, pp. 13 f.

by Jewish reckoning the beginning of Nisan 15th. This, if historically true, would be in itself a strong argument in favour of its having been an observance of the Passover. Those who follow the Johannine chronology do so because of difficulties in the Synoptic accounts. According to the Fourth Gospel, Jesus was crucified on the afternoon of Nisan 14th, when the paschal lambs were being sacrificed in the temple. He therefore died before the Passover meal was held in the evening of that day, by Jewish reckoning the beginning of Nisan 15th. Since, therefore, the meal which he had shared with the disciples the night before could not have been a Passover celebration, the followers of the Fourth Gospel on this point have to search for alternative explanations of the nature of that meal. The result is a number of hypotheses which have little or nothing in their favour.

We shall consider briefly these alternative views of what the Last Supper was, and then return to the difficulties which have been found in the Synoptic delineation of it as a Passover meal.

At the beginning of the sabbath or of a festival it was customary for the head of a household to say a prayer of sanctification (*kiddush*) of the day over a cup of wine which was drunk by him and the others who were present. Upon this has been built the sabbath *kiddush* theory, according to which Jesus and the twelve disciples formed a religious fellowship or *haburah*, like the so-called *haburoth* which are said to have held weekly meals on Friday afternoons, concluding with the *kiddush* of the sabbath.[1] Box (in the article in *The Jewish Guardian* mentioned in the last footnote) suggested that on this occasion the weekly meal was put back to Thursday because the next day Jesus and the disciples would have to be at the temple when the lambs were presented for sacrifice. But the sabbath *kiddush* always took place on Friday evening after sunset, i.e. at the commencement of the sabbath, and not twenty-four hours earlier.

[1] G. H. Box, 'The Jewish Antecedents of the Eucharist' in *Journal of Theological Studies*, iii, 1902, pp. 357-369, and 'The Jewish Background of the Institution of the Eucharist' in *The Jewish Guardian*, Dec. 7th, 1923; cf. also F. Spitta, *Zur Geschichte und Litteratur des Urchristentums*, i, 1893, p. 247.

The Nature of the Last Supper

A modification of this view is the Passover *kiddush* theory.[1] The gathering in the upper room is again like the *haburoth*. The customary weekly afternoon meal was interrupted at dusk for the sanctification ceremony, 'and as it was the eve of the Passover feast, it took the usual form of the combined commemoration of the Sabbath and the redemption from the Egyptian bondage, i.e. Passover *Kiddûsh*'.[2] The fatal flaw is that the Last Supper was held on a Thursday, not a Friday. It is suggested, however, that on this occasion the weekly meal was put back a day because of the sacrificing of the lambs on Friday afternoon. The answer to this is that the sanctification of the Passover cannot take place twenty-four hours before its commencement. It is the opening of the Passover meal and is said over the first cup.[3]

Another view, advocated by Lietzmann and others,[4] is a variation of the theory that Jesus and his disciples formed a religious association. According to this view, the Last Supper was an ordinary meal, and it has the advantage over the *kiddush* theories that the meal has not to be antedated by twenty-four hours. But although E. Gaugler[5] criticizes Jeremias for going too far in questioning the possibility of the holding by these associations of such ordinary meals as the Last Supper would have been,[6] the latter has shown that the *haburah* was an association of a particular kind, concerned with the observance of the Torah and with the performance of religious duties including attendance at special ritual meals held in connection with circumcisions, engagements,

---

[1] W. O. E. Oesterley, *The Jewish Background of the Christian Liturgy*, 1925, pp. 167 ff; G. H. C. Macgregor, *Eucharistic Origins*, 1928, pp. 44 ff; F. Gavin, *The Jewish Antecedents of the Christian Sacraments*, 1928, pp. 64 ff; and others.

[2] Oesterley, op. cit., p. 172.

[3] Mishnah, *Pesahim* 10.2; J. Jeremias, *Die Abendmahlsworte Jesu*, 2nd edn., 1949, p. 25. Some support is claimed for these two theories from the order cup–bread in the shorter text of Luke (22.15-19a), in 1 Cor. 10.16, 21, and in the *Didache*. But the last two cannot be used in this way, and the (first) cup in Luke (22.17) is the *kiddush* cup of a Passover meal.

[4] H. Lietzmann, *Messe und Herrenmahl*, 1926, pp. 202 ff, 228; F. L. Cirlot, *The Early Eucharist*, 1939, pp. 15 f, 44, 156; R. Otto, *The Kingdom of God and the Son of Man*, Eng. tr., 1943, p. 278; G. Dix, *The Shape of the Liturgy*, 2nd edn., 1945, pp. 50 ff.; J. E. L. Oulton, *Holy Communion and Holy Spirit*, 1951, pp. 9 ff.

[5] *Das Abendmahl im Neuen Testament*, 1943, p. 30, n. 3.

[6] J. Jeremias, *Die Abendmahlsworte Jesu*, 1st edn., 1935; see p. 26 in the 2nd edn., 1949.

weddings, and funerals. There is no evidence of any other meals being held by these *haburoth*; moreover, Jesus and his circle clearly did not form a regular association of this kind.

Attempts have been made to solve the problem by harmonizing John and the Synoptic Gospels. We need only mention here that of Billerbeck,[1] according to whom both John and the Synoptics are right, because in the year of the crucifixion Jesus and his disciples followed the Pharisees in eating the Passover a day earlier than the Sadducees. The Synoptics follow the Pharisaic reckoning, the Fourth Gospel the Sadducaic.[2]

Finally may be mentioned a solution proposed by Théo Preiss.[3] He follows the Johannine chronology, according to which the Last Supper was not a Passover meal. Accordingly Luke 22.15 ('I have earnestly desired to eat this Passover with you before I suffer') is interpreted (as by some other scholars) to mean that Jesus had wished to eat this Passover, but knew that he would be prevented by death from doing so. He transferred his hopes to the future, to the Messianic banquet in the Kingdom and to reunion there with his friends. He held a meal on the Thursday evening, the eve of his death, which, while not a Passover, had a paschal character and was an anticipation of the meal in the Kingdom. It is the paschal character of this last meal which has caused the erroneous Synoptic chronology, in which the Last Supper has become an actual Passover. This solution of the problem is quite unconvincing.

It is clear from this brief review that the various attempts to supplant the Synoptic chronology and to explain the Last Supper as something other than a celebration of the Passover are all attended by grave difficulties. It is felt, however, by champions of the Johannine account of the matter, that equally grave objections can be levelled against the Synoptic representation of the

[1] Strack-Billerbeck, *Kommentar zum Neuen Testament aus Talmud und Midrasch*, ii, 1924, pp. 847-853.
[2] This attractive theory is nothing more than a bare possibility, with no real evidence in its support; cf. J. Jeremias, op. cit., 2nd edn., 1949, p. 15.
[3] 'Le dernier repas de Jésus fut-il un repas pascal?' in *Theologische Zeitschrift*, iv, 2 (March-April 1948), pp. 81-101.

The Nature of the Last Supper

Last Supper as a Passover. To the chief of these objections we now turn.[1]

1. It is urged that if the Last Supper had been a Passover, the unleavened bread would have been given its proper name, ἄζυμα, whereas our accounts (Mark 14.22 parr.; 1 Cor. 11.23) use ἄρτος, the word for ordinary bread. It is quite certain, however, that ἄρτος was also used to denote unleavened bread.

2. In the accounts no mention is made of the paschal lamb and the bitter herbs. The narratives, however, even the most primitive in form, that of Mark, are to be regarded not as verbatim records of every detail of the gathering in the upper room, but primarily as cultic formulae which reflect the liturgical practice of the early Church. That is why emphasis is laid on the bread and wine and the words spoken about them by Jesus, to the exclusion of other details which were of the first importance in any Passover meal, but had no place at all in the Church's Eucharist.

3. Another objection is that our accounts speak of a common cup, whereas, it is alleged, at the Passover, individual cups were used. But the probabilities are in favour of the use of the common cup in the time of Jesus.

4. A contradiction is found in Mark 14.1 f (followed by Matt. 26.1-5): 'And after two days was the Passover and the Unleavened Bread. And the chief priests and the scribes were seeking how to arrest him by stealth and kill him. For they said, Not during the feast (μὴ ἐν τῇ ἑορτῇ), lest there be a tumult of the people.' According to the Markan account, however, Jesus *was* arrested during the feast, on the night of Nisan 15th. This, it is thought, must be a mistake, and it is the indication of time in Mark 14.1 f which is correct. But it has recently been argued by Jeremias[2] that the words μὴ ἐν τῇ ἑορτῇ do not bear the meaning usually given them, for pilgrims were already present in Jerusalem sev-

---

[1] The chief authorities for the identification of the Last Supper as a Passover meal are: G. Dalman, *Jesus-Jeshua*, Eng. tr., 1929, pp. 86-132; Strack-Billerbeck, op. cit., ii, 1924, pp. 812 ff; iv, 1928, pp. 41ff; and Jeremias, op. cit., pp. 10-49, to the last of which in particular I am greatly indebted in what follows. Jeremias' arguments are summarized in his article 'The Last Supper' in *Journal of Theological Studies*, i, 1949, pp. 1-10.   [2] Op. cit., pp. 40-42.

eral days before the feast. The arrest was to be secret, and not openly among the crowd up for the festival, 'not in the presence of the festival crowd'.

5. The main objection is based on a series of events which, it is claimed, could not possibly have taken place on the festival day, Nisan 15th.

(*a*) Jesus went to Gethsemane on Passover night (Mark 14.26, 32 parr.), whereas it was not permissible to leave Jerusalem on that night. The answer to this is that Gethsemane, at the western foot of the Mount of Olives, was reckoned within the confines of the city for the purposes of the Passover.[1]

(*b*) The carrying of arms (Luke 22.38; Mark 14.43, 47, 48 parr.) was forbidden on a festival. This commonly repeated statement is incorrect, for on sabbaths and festival days arms were permitted to soldiers, and to ordinary people as part of their attire for self-defence.[2]

(*c*) One of the weightiest arguments against the authenticity of the Synoptic representation of the crucifixion as having occurred on Nisan 15th is undoubtedly that which concerns the session of the sanhedrin and the condemnation of Jesus to death on the very night of the Passover. Certainly the Rabbinical law forbids judging on feast days,[3] but it forbids trials of capital crimes also on the eve of a sabbath or feast day,[4] because the verdict, if a conviction, had to be postponed till the day after the trial. So this tells just as much against the Johannine as against the Synoptic chronology. Jeremias says: 'But in the case of Jesus there intervened an ordinance of the Torah itself. In a few cases of heinous crimes Deuteronomy [17.13] commands that the death sentence should be published as a deterrent; as it says: "And all Israel shall hear and fear." All the people being gathered *only* at the three pilgrim festivals (Passover, Pentecost, Tabernacles), this commandment was interpreted by the Rabbis to the effect that, in spite of the prohibition of executions on festivals, in these few

---

[1] See also G. Dalman, op. cit., pp. 93-95. [2] Id., pp. 96 f.
[3] Mishnah, *Betzah* 5.2. [4] Mishnah, *Sanhedrin* 4.1.

The Nature of the Last Supper

special cases enumerated in Deuteronomy the death penalty must be carried out at the feast. One of these cases was that of a false prophet. Jesus being a false prophet in the eyes of his adversaries, his condemnation had to take place immediately, in order that the execution could be carried out on 15th Nisan. For only on this day were the people assembled; on 16th Nisan people were allowed to return home, unless it was a sabbath.'[1]

Of course, the Jews did not carry out the execution, although they were anxious that the Romans should do so. Since it was taken out of their hands, the question of the actual crucifixion on the feast day does not concern Jewish regulations. For this reason it seems to me that Jeremias' explanation about Jesus being regarded as a false prophet is unnecessary. The Jews would not have allowed a scruple against the holding of a session of the sanhedrin on a technically illegal day to stand in the way of their eagerness to have Jesus removed from the scene.

(d) The coming of Simon of Cyrene ἀπ' ἀγροῦ, 'from the country' (Mark 15.21; Luke 23.26) can be urged as a relevant objection to the Synoptic account only if he was a Jew and had been working in the fields on the festival day, which was, of course, forbidden. But he may not have been a Jew, and if he was, he would hardly have been coming from work so early in the day, about 9 a.m. (cf. Mark 15.25), but may merely have been coming from his home outside the city[2] to attend the morning service at the temple.

(e) The purchase of the linen by Joseph of Arimathaea on the evening of the festival is alleged to be impossible. In fact only Mark 15.46 actually mentions the purchase of the linen; but there is nothing impossible about it. Although buying and selling were forbidden on sabbaths and feast days, exceptions were made in cases of real need, including a death; one could buy coffin and linen (but not fix the price),[3] because the hot Palestinian climate made early burial necessary.

---

[1] *Journal of Theological Studies*, i, 1949, p. 6. Jeremias gives the details in *Die Abendmahlsworte Jesu*, 2nd edn., 1949, p. 44.
[2] ἀπ' ἀγροῦ can mean 'from a farm'; cf. G. Dalman, op. cit., pp. 100 f.
[3] Babylonian Talmud, *Shabbath* 151a; Tosephta, *Shabbath* 17.13.

(f) It is objected that the taking down of the body from the cross and the burial were not possible on a feast day. It was, however, perfectly possible, even on a feast day, especially in view of Deut. 21.22 f, where the reason is that the land should not be defiled.[1]

There is thus nothing in the Synoptic accounts which really invalidates their representation of the Last Supper as a Passover meal and of the crucifixion as having taken place on the first day of the festival, Nisan 15th.

There are, however, more positive indications that the Last Supper was a Passover. I give the most telling of these.[2]

1. The Last Supper took place in the evening and extended into the night.[3] The usual main meal of the day was taken in the late afternoon, but it was obligatory for the Passover to be eaten at night.[4]

2. Jesus and his disciples reclined at their last meal together (Mark 14.18; Matt. 26.20; Luke 22.14; John 13.12, 23, 25, 28), whereas the Jews in the time of Jesus sat at ordinary meals. The Israelites had been slaves in Egypt, and it was a Passover ordinance that they should recline as a symbol of their liberty.[5]

3. A dish precedes the breaking of bread only at the Passover. This *hors d'oeuvre* consists of green herbs, bitter herbs, and fruit sauce (*haroseth*), a mixture of dried fruits, spices, and vinegar. Thus the Mishnah says: 'When food is brought before him he eats it seasoned with lettuce, until he is come to the breaking of bread'.[6] This preliminary dish is referred to in Mark 14.20 and Matt. 26.23, and the meal is already in progress (Mark 14.18;

---

[1] Dalman, op. cit., pp. 103 f, remarks: 'Even Jewish traditional Law would have had nothing to say against the legality of this interment, if the purchase of the grave clothes was in accordance with the Jewish enactments.'

[2] Here are deliberately left out of account the *explicit* identifications of the supper with the Passover (Mark 14.12, 14, 16 parr.; Luke 22.15), which might be and sometimes have been regarded as a construction of the evangelists.

[3] All the Gospels and Paul agree on this point: Mark 14.17; Matt. 26.20; Mark 14.30 parr.; John 13.30; 1 Cor. 11.23. Luke's explicit description of the meal as a Passover means, of course, that it took place at night.

[4] Ex. 12.8; *Jub.* 49.1, 12; Mishnah, *Zebahim* 5.8; cf. Mishnah, *Pesahim* 5.10.

[5] Jerusalem Talmud, *Pesahim* 10.1.

[6] *Pesahim* 10.3.

The Nature of the Last Supper

Matt. 26.21) when Jesus takes bread and offers a blessing and breaks the bread.[1]

4. Wine was drunk at the Last Supper, and the drinking of wine was obligatory at the Passover. That this was an old custom is evident from its being taken for granted in the Book of Jubilees (end of the second century B.C.), which contains the first mention of it (49.6, 9).[2] Wine was, of course, drunk on other festive occasions, but at the Passover the wine was *red*.[3] That the wine at the Last Supper was red is proved by the comparison of it with blood by our Lord.

5. The Last Supper concluded with the singing of a hymn (Mark 14.26; Matt. 26.30), which will have been the second part (Pss. 114-or 115-118) of the Hallel which closed the Passover meal.[4]

6. After the meal Jesus did not return, according to his custom, to Bethany, but went to the Mount of Olives. This was in accord with the Passover regulation that after the Passover had been eaten within the walls of Jerusalem, the rest of the night might be spent inside a larger area, which excluded Bethany but included Gethsemane.

7. A suggestion of considerable force is that the very fact that Jesus spoke of his body and blood in connection with the bread and wine is an indication of the Passover character of the Last Supper, because in the Passover Haggadah the person presiding explained the various elements in the meal. Not that the words of institution replaced these customary explanations; rather they were suggested by them. They were spoken at the distribution of the bread and wine, while the Passover Haggadah preceded the meal proper.

It remains to say a few words at this point about the Fourth

---

[1] The words καὶ ἐσθιόντων αὐτῶν in Mark 14.22 (cf. Matt. 26.26) immediately before the words of institution are probably secondary, and a repetition of those in verse 18.

[2] Cf. Mishnah, *Pesahim* 10.1.

[3] References in Jeremias, op. cit., p. 106.

[4] In support of this identification is the interesting fact that the Greek word in Mark and Matthew (ὑμνεῖν) for the singing at the end of the meal corresponds to a loan-word (*hiymnon*) which is sometimes used as a name for the Hallel in Rabbinical literature; see Strack-Billerbeck, op. cit., iv, 1928, p. 76.

Gospel. While this Gospel antedates the Last Supper by twenty-four hours so that Jesus becomes the true paschal lamb, suffering death at the time of the slaughtering of the lambs in the temple, there are not lacking indications that the evangelist depends on a tradition which resembles the Synoptics in understanding the Last Supper as a Passover meal. Indeed, Jeremias[1] goes so far as to assert that the only certain place for the Johannine dating is 18.28, where the Jews refused to enter the praetorium 'that they might not be defiled, but might eat the Passover'; 13.1 simply states that Jesus knew before the Passover that his death was near; and in 19.14 παρασκευὴ τοῦ πάσχα may mean not 'the preparation of the Passover', but 'Friday of Passover week'. In John, as in the other Gospels, the Last Supper is a night meal (13.30), the guests recline (13.23, 28), and afterwards go, not to Bethany, but across the Kidron valley (18.1, i.e. to the Mount of Olives). Then there is 13.26-30, a passage peculiar to the Fourth Gospel. It was natural that in later tradition the actual traitor Judas should be mentioned, as in Matt. 26.25; but John goes further. Verse 29 reads, 'For some thought that, because Judas had the money-box, Jesus was telling him, Buy what we need for the feast; or, that he should give something to the poor'. This seems inconsistent. While Jeremias[2] points to a possible reference to almsgiving at the Passover in the second alternative view of what Jesus said, the first alternative view does not allow the meal to be a Passover, since it is clearly already in progress, and therefore it is much too late to talk about acquiring what was needed for it. Not much reliance can be placed upon this passage, unless we suppose that the last part of verse 29 belongs to a tradition in which the Last Supper was a Passover, but has been combined with the evangelist's transformed chronology without the removal of the inconsistency.[3] We conclude that while the fourth evangelist, for

---

[1] Op. cit., p. 46.   [2] Op. cit., p. 29.
[3] John 19.31 as it stands certainly seems to agree with the Johannine chronology, i.e. the sabbath is a 'great day' because it coincides with Nisan 15th, the first day of Unleavened Bread. But the Passover is not mentioned here any more than in verse 42, where παρασκευή means Friday. It is therefore possible that in the tradition from which 19.31-37 comes παρασκευή meant simply Friday, and that the sabbath was a

The Nature of the Last Supper

theological reasons, antedates the chronology by twenty-four hours, he depends on a tradition (or traditions) which agrees with the Synoptics in regarding the Last Supper as a Passover, and in placing the crucifixion on Nisan 15th.

The objection has often been brought forward that if, as the Synoptics suggest, the Last Supper was a Passover, it is very strange that we find no mention of the paschal lamb or the bitter herbs. It is of the utmost importance to be clear about the nature of the Synoptic accounts (and that of Paul); and this chapter may close with a re-emphasis of what has already been suggested earlier. What is given is not a description in detail of the last earthly meal of Jesus with his disciples, but an account of the first Eucharist, the institution of the Church's Eucharist as it first began to be celebrated after the resurrection. Because of the special words of explanation uniquely attached by Jesus to the bread and wine, these elements of the meal replaced the lamb as the central feature, and so gave rise to a rite quite different from the annual Passover, to a daily or weekly gathering for the 'breaking of bread'.[1]

'great day' because it coincided with Nisan 16th, which could also be called 'great' because on it, according to the Pharisaic tradition, the offering of the *omer*, the first sheaf of barley must be made (Lev. 23.10 f, 15). 'The morrow after the sabbath' was taken by the Pharisees to mean the second day of Passover, while the Sadducees more naturally thought the literal sabbath in Passover week was meant; see L. Finkelstein, *The Pharisees*, 1946, pp. 115-117 and n. 24; Strack-Billerbeck, op. cit., ii, 1924, pp. 847 f. If this is so, the tradition utilized by the evangelist originally agreed with the Synoptic chronology. Cf. R. Bultmann, *Das Evangelium des Johannes*, 1950 (=1941), p. 524, n. 5.

[1] Among recent supporters of the view that the Last Supper was a Passover are: E. Gaugler, *Das Abendmahl im Neuen Testament*, 1943; M. Barth, *Das Abendmahl: Passamahl, Bundesmahl, und Messiasmahl*, 1945; F. J. Leenhardt, *Le sacrement de la sainte cène*, 1948; E. Stauffer, *Die Theologie des Neuen Testaments*, 4th edn., 1948, pp. 141 f. It is only fair to add that some hesitations remain in the minds even of strong advocates of our view. Thus Gaugler (pp. 24 f) does not think that the arguments of Jeremias, Dalman, and Billerbeck amount to *proofs* of the thesis, and regards as serious difficulties the session of the sanhedrin on the night of the Passover, and the execution of Jesus on the first day of the feast. E. Lohmeyer, who decided against the identification of the Last Supper as a Passover in favour of an analogy with the *kiddush* practice, also judged the arguments of Jeremias (in *Die Abendmahlsworte Jesu*, 1st edn., 1935) to be indecisive ('Vom urchristlichen Abendmahl' in *Theologische Rundschau*, ix, 1937, p. 198). Opposition to the view that the Last Supper was a Passover has many vigorous champions. The veteran M. Goguel, for instance, in his recent book *L'église primitive*, 1948, pp. 348 f, still maintains the position adopted in his classic treatment of the subject, *L'eucharistie des origines à Justin Martyr*, 1910, pp. 62-65. But Lietzmann (op. cit., p. 212) went too far in asserting that the paschal theory of the Last Supper has not 'a glimmer of probability' about it.

CHAPTER THREE

THE EUCHARISTIC SAYINGS OF JESUS: THEIR FORM

THE texts to be considered are: Matt. 26.26-29, Mark 14.22-25, 1 Cor. 11.23-25, and Luke 22.15-20.

1. *Matthew*

Matthew's narrative of the Last Supper can quickly be disposed of, as it is merely an expanded and more liturgical form of Mark's account. Thus we may note the addition of 'eat' after 'take'; the parallel command to drink ('drink ye all from it') instead of Mark's statement that the disciples all drank of the cup; the reason for the command to drink ('for this is my blood', etc.); the blood is shed 'for the remission of sins'.

2. *Mark and Paul*

Paul's narrative of the Last Supper in 1 Cor., which was written in the early fifties, is certainly our earliest written account. But that of the Gospel of Mark, which was written about two decades later, is shown by its Aramaisms to be more primitive than Paul's version.[1] They are independent narratives, but descended from the same original tradition.[2] Here, however, arises a real difficulty, for Paul introduces his narrative of the Last Supper with the statement: 'For I received from the Lord that which

[1] For an excellent discussion of the Semitisms in Mark's account see J. Jeremias, *Die Abendmahlsworte Jesu*, 2nd edn., 1949, pp. 88-94. ἐκχυννόμενον Mark 14.24 is the futuristic use of the Aramaic participle, referring to the imminent shedding of the blood of Jesus; in ὑπὲρ πολλῶν, πολλοί has its often inclusive sense of 'all'—the blood will be shed for the nations, 'for all'. Of particular significance are the Semitisms in Mark 14.25 (which is not repeated by Paul), especially τοῦ γενήματος τῆς ἀμπέλου, wine being called 'the fruit of the vine' also in the Jewish benediction over wine.

[2] H. Lietzmann, *Messe und Herrenmahl*, 1926, pp. 218, 227; J. Jeremias, op. cit., p. 94; cf. also E. Gaugler, *Das Abendmahl im Neuen Testament*, 1943, p. 17.

The Eucharistic Sayings of Jesus: their Form

also I delivered to you' (ἐγὼ γὰρ παρέλαβον ἀπὸ τοῦ κυρίου, ὃ καὶ παρέδωκα ὑμῖν), a statement which might be taken to mean that Paul's version of the tradition was superior to any other, such as that in Mark, from which it differs in important respects.

One view of Paul's statement, now rejected by most scholars,[1] is that it means that the apostle received his account of the institution of the Lord's Supper by direct revelation, just as in Gal. 1.12 he declares that he received his Gospel not from men, but 'through revelation of Jesus Christ', alluding to his encounter with the risen Christ on the road to Damascus. If, however, the Lord in 1 Cor. 11.23 is the *direct* source of information, the preposition in the phrase 'from the Lord' would more naturally be not ἀπό, but παρά, as in Gal. 1.12 (παρὰ ἀνθρώπου, 'from man').[2] We must also take into account the closely similar passage 1 Cor. 15.3-5, where Paul is handing on the Church tradition he had received concerning the resurrection of the Lord, and where the same two words are used for the delivering and receiving of the tradition as in 1 Cor. 11.23.[3] The probability is, then, that in our passage Paul is not suggesting that the account of the institution of the Lord's Supper which he is about to give was the subject of a special revelation vouchsafed to him.[4]

A second view, that of Lietzmann, is that Paul received in a vision by special revelation the real meaning of the Eucharist as a commemoration of the death of Christ. The substance of the revelation is the command to 'do this in remembrance of me'. Paul, by emphasizing the atoning death of Christ, was the real originator of a type of Eucharist which differed from the so-called

---

[1] It was held by A. Loisy, *Les évangiles synoptiques*, ii, 1908, p. 532, n. 1; cf. *The Birth of the Christian Religion*, Eng. tr., 1948, pp. 244 f.

[2] ἀπό is, however, sometimes used like παρά in this sense, e.g. Col. 1.7. But that the difficulty was early felt is shown by the fact that DE read παρά (FG have ἀπὸ θεοῦ).

[3] J. Jeremias, op. cit., p. 96 shows that the language of the *kerygma* in 1 Cor. 15.3-5 is un-Pauline, and betrays signs of Aramaic origin.

[4] Among recent writers F. J. Leenhardt (*Le sacrement de la sainte cène*, 1948, p. 51) does not absolutely exclude the revelation theory, though he thinks it much more likely that the phrase 'I received from the Lord' denotes a tradition which goes back to Jesus.

The Lord's Supper in the New Testament

Jerusalem type.[1] W. G. Kümmel, in his note on p. 185 of Lietzmann's commentary, dissents from Lietzmann's view, holding that Paul regarded himself as handing on unaltered the Church tradition which ultimately goes back to the Lord. This view is shared by most scholars, among whom may be mentioned M. Goguel,[2] J. Weiss,[3] A. Schweitzer,[4] M. Dibelius,[5] F. L. Cirlot,[6] E. Gaugler,[7] Théo Preiss,[8] R. Bultmann,[9] and J. Héring.[10] Paul is in the position of a Christian Rabbi, handing on to others the tradition he has himself received. The words he uses ($\pi\alpha\rho\alpha\lambda\alpha\mu\beta\acute{\alpha}\nu\epsilon\iota\nu$ and $\pi\alpha\rho\alpha\delta\iota\delta\acute{o}\nu\alpha\iota$) are the equivalents of the Rabbinical terms ($qibbel$ and $masar$) for the reception and transmission of tradition.[11]

E. Lohmeyer, in opposing Lietzmann's theory that the command 'do this in remembrance of me' forms the essence of the new emphasis on the nature of the Eucharist which was specially revealed to Paul, points out that the language both of this sentence and of the whole account is un-Pauline.[12] The word for 'remembrance' ($\dot{\alpha}\nu\acute{\alpha}\mu\nu\eta\sigma\iota\varsigma$) is not used by Paul elsewhere.[13] The term 'the Lord Jesus' in narrative is also peculiar. Most telling of all is the word for the 'body' of Jesus, $\sigma\hat{\omega}\mu\alpha$, which Paul elsewhere applies to the Church as the body of Christ. The very

---

[1] See H. Lietzmann, op. cit., p. 255, and *An die Korinther I-II*, 4th edn. (edited with additional notes by W. G. Kümmel), 1949, p. 57. Lietzmann is followed slavishly here, as in so much else, by A. B. Macdonald, *Christian Worship in the Primitive Church*, 1934, pp. 143 f.
[2] *L'eucharistie des origines à Justin Martyr*, 1910, p. 161.
[3] *Der erste Korintherbrief*, 10th edn., 1925, p. 283.
[4] *The Mysticism of Paul the Apostle*, Eng. tr., 1931, pp. 173, 266 f.
[5] *From Tradition to Gospel*, Eng. tr., 1934, pp. 205 f. Dibelius regards Paul's tradition as that current in the Greek-speaking churches of Antioch and Damascus to which 'Paul had adhered when he became a Christian'.
[6] *The Early Eucharist*, 1939, pp. 143 f.
[7] Op. cit., p. 15.
[8] 'Le dernier repas de Jésus fut-il un repas pascal?' in *Theologische Zeitschrift*, iv, 2 (March-April 1948), p. 87.
[9] *Theologie des Neuen Testaments*, i, 1948, pp. 148 f.
[10] *La première épître de saint Paul aux Corinthiens*, 1949, p. 100.
[11] Strack-Billerbeck, *Kommentar zum Neuen Testament aus Talmud und Midrasch*, iii, 1926, p. 444.
[12] 'Vom urchristlichen Abendmahl' in *Theologische Rundschau*, ix, 1937, pp. 183 f.
[13] The same is true, Lohmeyer points out, of $\dot{o}\sigma\acute{a}\kappa\iota\varsigma$ ('as often as') in verses 25 and 26. But it should be noticed that the presence of this word in the latter verse, which is certainly not from the tradition, but a remark of the apostle, suggests that 'as often as you drink it' is an insertion by Paul into the second injunction to repeat the rite, which itself is most probably Pauline.

The Eucharistic Sayings of Jesus: their Form

fact that in 1 Cor. 10.16 f Paul combines these two meanings of σῶμα indicates that its presence in the narrative of the Last Supper suggested the special meaning he attached to it.[1] The form of the narrative is determined by liturgical usage; it is an *ätiologischer Kultbericht*.[2] No doubt the same is true, though to a lesser degree, of the Markan version.

Which of these two independent traditions, the Markan and the Pauline, is to be preferred? Which of them offers us the sayings of Jesus in their more original form? On the one hand, that of Mark is the more primitive; on the other, Paul claims for his form of the tradition the ultimate authority of the Lord himself. We must consider further the deeper meaning and the implications of Paul's claim to have received what he relates 'from the Lord'.

If Paul had written only 'I received from the Lord that the Lord Jesus on the night', etc., it would have been necessary to take him to mean that he was reproducing the actual words of Jesus, whereas 'the fact that he speaks of his delivering a tradition means that he is possibly giving his own version of what he has received'.[3] In the transmission of Rabbinic tradition what was handed down from one generation to another was the substance and explanation of the Torah ('a kind of fixed deposit'), which had been directly communicated by God to the first member in the series. 'Similarly', W. D. Davies writes, 'we are not to understand from Paul's account of the Last Supper that he is quoting the *ipsissima verba* of Jesus, but we are to find there the precipitate of those words percolated through the mind of a Rabbi. . . . This approach to Paul's account makes it possible for us to understand why it is, as has often been pointed out, that the essential meaning of the Markan and Pauline accounts is the same while it is the formulation that differs.' In Davies' neat phrase the Pauline formulation (in particular of the cup saying) is 'a Rabbinization of the tradition'.[4]

---

[1] Cf. J. Jeremias, op. cit., p. 97, who assigns 1 Cor. 11.23-25 to the Antiochene tradition.   [2] E. Lohmeyer, op. cit., p. 185.
[3] W. D. Davies, *Paul and Rabbinic Judaism*, 1948, p. 249.   [4] Id., p. 250.

The Lord's Supper in the New Testament

Relevant here also is what O. Cullmann has written in an instructive study entitled ' "KYRIOS" as Designation for the Oral Tradition concerning Jesus (*Paradosis* and *Kyrios*)'.[1] He calls attention to certain passages (1 Cor. 7.10, 25; 9.14; 1 Thess. 4.15) in which 'the Lord' occupies the place of 'tradition', and to the combination of these in 1 Cor. 11.23, 'I received (by tradition) from the Lord'. 'The Lord' here is not only the historical Jesus as the chronological source of the tradition, but the exalted Lord behind the transmission of the tradition, who works *in* it. Thus 'ἀπὸ τοῦ Κυρίου can mean a direct[2] receiving from the Lord, without it being necessary to think of a vision or of excluding middle members through whom the Lord Himself imparts the *paradosis*'.[3]

The conclusion is that it is possible for Paul in 1 Cor. 11.23 in all sincerity to attribute the tradition he has received to the Lord himself, and at the same time to interpret, and consequently even to modify the tradition, though not in a sense contrary to its original meaning, and to attribute this also to the Lord, and to the apostolic tradition through which the Lord transmits his words and deeds.

The significant differences between the Markan and Pauline accounts of the Last Supper are four-fold, and concern:

(*a*) The saying over the bread.

(*b*) The saying over the cup.

(*c*) The absence from Mark of the command to repeat.

(*d*) The absence from the Pauline version of the eschatological saying in Mark 14.25.

(*a*) *The saying over the bread*

Mark 14.22. 'Take; this is my body.'

1 Cor. 11.24. 'This is my body which is for you.'

---

[1] In *Scottish Journal of Theology*, iii, 2 (June 1950), pp. 180-197.
[2] See Col. 1.7 for an example of this less common use of ἀπό.
[3] Id., p. 189. This interesting suggestion has the advantage of removing a possible difficulty, that strictly παραλαμβάνειν should denote *direct* reception of tradition; see Davies, op. cit., p. 249.

The Eucharistic Sayings of Jesus: their Form

Paul's addition 'which is for you' must be a secondary Hellenization, as it cannot be retranslated into Aramaic.[1] That it was early felt to be harsh also in Greek is shown by the addition of participles in certain authorities.[2] According to J. Weiss[3] it is a 'haggadistic addition' in explanation of the saying of Jesus about his body. He attributes it to Paul, who is explaining the meaning he himself would attach to the cultic practice of the breaking of bread. Paul is not conscious, however, of adding anything to the traditional utterance of Jesus, but is making clear what he holds to be its essential meaning. This may be so. But it is equally possible that the words already stood in the tradition received by Paul, and that their presence is due to their being more suitable in worship and more intelligible to Hellenistic communities than the Semitic phrase, 'which is poured out for *many*' which follows the cup saying in Mark. In other words, the two phrases, one of them attached to the saying over the bread, and the other to that over the cup, are variants of an original tradition.

(*b*) *The saying over the cup*

Mark 14.24. 'This is my blood of the covenant which is poured out for many.'

1 Cor. 11.25. 'This cup is the new covenant in my blood.'

Here the differences are manifestly much greater than in the case of the saying over the bread, and it might even be felt that 'it is beyond our power to determine which is the more original form'.[4]

The often felt difficulty in the Greek of the phrase 'my blood of the covenant' in Mark may be deferred for the moment. Serious objection has been taken, especially from the Jewish side, to its meaning and to the possibility that Jesus enjoined the drinking

---

[1] G. Dalman, *Jesus-Jeshua*, Eng. tr., 1929, pp. 144 f. Moreover, it would be difficult to explain Mark's omission of these words if they were authentic.

[2] κλώμενον ('broken') FG, many minuscules, some Old Latin manuscripts, Peshitta, Harkleian Syriac; θρυπτόμενον ('crushed') D; διδόμενον ('given') Vulgate, Coptic, Armenian (as in Luke 22.19).

[3] Op. cit., pp. 285 f.

[4] R. Newton Flew, *Jesus and His Church*, 2nd edn., 1943, p. 72.

of wine as in some sense representing his blood. The Jewish scholar C. G. Montefiore in his commentary on Mark wrote of the difficulty of believing 'that a Palestinian or Galilaean Jew could have suggested that in drinking wine his disciples were, even symbolically, drinking blood. For the horror with which the drinking of blood was regarded by the Jews is well known'.[1] Similarly H. Loewe writes: 'Jews shudder at certain passages in Hebrews and Romans, and the Gospel verses describing the institution of the Eucharist are painfully repugnant to them.'[2] There are obvious answers to these objections.[3] But such feelings have led to the view that the Markan form of this saying originated in a non-Jewish community, and that the Pauline form is the earlier.[4]

The most recent author of a work devoted to the New Testament Eucharist to hold to the priority of the Pauline account is F. J. Leenhardt.[5] The Pauline version of the saying over the cup is, in his opinion, pre-Pauline, and represents the thought of Jesus in which the idea of covenant as the preparation for participation in the Kingdom of God was central. The cup is the sign and pledge of a share in the new covenant, and so in the Kingdom.[6] The *formule bâtarde* of Mark is the result of a liturgical tendency to make the saying symmetrical with that about the bread, and

---

[1] *The Synoptic Gospels*, i, 1927, p. 332. Drinking of blood was forbidden because 'the life of the flesh is in the blood', and because it was a means of atonement; cf. Lev. 17.10-12.

[2] *A Rabbinic Anthology*, 1938, p. 647; cf. J. Klausner, *Jesus of Nazareth*, Eng. tr., 1947 (=1925), p. 329, who thinks it 'quite impossible' for Jesus to have invited his disciples to eat of his body and drink of his blood.

[3] See, e.g. V. Taylor, *Jesus and His Sacrifice*, 1943 (=1937), pp. 134 f, whose remarks include the reminder that 'Jesus does not invite His disciples to drink blood, or to drink blood symbolically, but to drink wine as representing His life surrendered for many'.

[4] So M. Dibelius, op. cit., p. 207.   [5] Op. cit., pp. 51 ff.

[6] The originality of the saying in Paul as against the Markan form is also upheld by J. Behm in his articles in G. Kittel's *Theologisches Wörterbuch zum Neuen Testament* on διαθήκη (ii, 1935, pp. 136 f—the blood or death of Jesus founds the new covenant, and so the wine represents the new covenant, the fulfilment of the prophecy of Jeremiah (31.31 ff)) and on κλάω (iii, 1938, p. 730); and by R. Newton Flew, op. cit., p. 72, n. 1, who observes (p. 75) that the living influence of the prophecy of Jeremiah in the time of Jesus is proved by the existence of the Damascus Sect who called themselves 'the men who entered into the new covenant in the land of Damascus' (*Fragments of a Zadokite Work*, 9.28).

The Eucharistic Sayings of Jesus: their Form

to assimilate it to Ex. 24.8 (LXX ἰδοὺ τὸ αἷμα τῆς διαθήκης, 'behold the blood of the covenant').[1] In other words, Jesus did not say 'This is my blood', but spoke rather of the covenant in his blood. In Mark the blood is the correlative of the body. But according to Leenhardt they are not true parallels; the correlative of blood would need to be flesh; and besides, Jesus had already referred implicitly to his blood in speaking of his body.

Leenhardt goes on to ask how the wine, according to Mark, could have been called his blood by Jesus, and then immediately afterwards be termed 'the fruit of the vine'. His reply is that while the latter comes from historical tradition, the evangelist is indebted for the former to liturgical usage.

Lastly, Leenhardt brings forward against Mark's report of the saying the very awkward construction of the Greek for 'my blood of the covenant'. It has already been decided to postpone consideration of this important point, but we may remark in anticipation that, while this criticism of the Markan form is perfectly justifiable, it is not derived from the Pauline form.

In answer to the position, as represented by Leenhardt, that the Pauline form of the word of Jesus over the cup is more reliable than that in Mark, it may firstly be conceded that the covenant idea may well have been to the fore in the thought of Jesus, if, as was surely the case, he envisaged a new people of God. Behm[2] thinks that the single occurrence of καινὴ διαθήκη (new covenant) in the teaching of Jesus is no argument against its authenticity, and that it is this very saying of Jesus which explains the centrality of the covenant idea in Paul (and Hebrews). I would urge, however, on the contrary, that it is much more likely that the importance of the covenant conception in Paul's thought (see Rom. 9.4; 11.27; 2 Cor. 3.6 ff; Gal. 3.15 ff; 4.24 ff; Eph. 2.12) has played its part in the formation of his variation of the cup saying.

Secondly, the reasoning that the true correlative of blood is

---

[1] So also Behm in the article on κλάω mentioned in the last footnote, p. 730.
[2] In G. Kittel's *Theologisches Wörterbuch zum Neuen Testament*, ii, 1935, p. 137.

not body, but flesh, and that Jesus did not say 'This is my blood', would be superfluous if, as is probable, 'body' stands for 'flesh' in this saying.¹ Thus 'This is my blood' would have as strong a claim to authenticity as 'This is my body', and the addition to it of the words 'of the covenant' under the influence of Ex. 24.8 is not a conscious alteration of what we find in Paul; rather, both the Markan and the Pauline versions are independent attempts to interpret the significance of the word of Jesus about his blood.

Thirdly, the reply to Leenhardt's reference to the two different descriptions of wine in Mark 14.24, 25 as unfavourable to the authenticity of 'This is my blood' is that it is probable that Luke more accurately preserves the tradition in placing the saying about the fruit of the vine at the beginning of the meal.

To turn more directly to the cup saying as reported by Mark, we have seen that the expression 'which is poured out for many' is Semitic in origin. There seems little doubt that it is a reminiscence of Isa. 53.12; Jesus is the Servant of the Lord who fulfils the role of one of whom the prophet declared that 'he poured out his soul unto death', and 'bore the sin of many'. The words 'This is my blood' are to be included among the actual utterances of Jesus who, believing himself to be the Servant of the Lord, told his disciples that his blood would be shed for many: 'This is my blood which is (to be) poured out for many (all)'.

The crux in Mark's form of this declaration is the expression 'my blood *of the covenant*' (τὸ αἷμά μου τῆς διαθήκης). The difficulties concern both language and content.

Even in Greek the expression is very harsh, and the true explanation seems to be that the words 'of the covenant' are a later addition to the reported utterance of Jesus intended as an interpretation of it in covenant terms. We find another interpretation in the Pauline version, where, however, the awkwardness of that in Mark is absent because 'the covenant' has become the predicate.²

---

[1] See below, p. 49, n. 2.
[2] We cannot follow R. Bultmann, op. cit., p. 144, in supposing that not only τῆς διαθήκης, but τὸ ἐκχυννόμενον (ὑπὲρ πολλῶν) is a subsequent interpretative addition in Mark.

The Eucharistic Sayings of Jesus: their Form

The genuineness of the words in question becomes still more doubtful when an attempt is made to retranslate them into Aramaic. Jeremias[1] goes so far as to say that this cannot be done, because Aramaic does not permit a noun with a personal pronoun ('my blood') to be followed by a genitive ('of the covenant'). Dalman, however, only says such an Aramaic phrase would be 'rather hard', but he is clearly not satisfied with the Greek as we have it.[2]

Again, the expression 'blood of the covenant' or 'covenant blood' in later Judaism signified rather the blood of circumcision (cf. Gen. 17.10)[3]—another factor telling against its correctness in the context of the Last Supper.

For these reasons we conclude that the words 'of the covenant' form no part of the original tradition of this saying of Jesus.

There still remains the question whether, nevertheless, Jesus did actually speak at the Last Supper of a covenant and, as Paul has it, of a *new* covenant—'This cup is the new covenant in my blood'. If Paul's form of this saying is correct, then Jesus viewed his coming death as establishing a covenant in fulfilment of Jer. 31.31 ff. There is, perhaps, some force in E. Gaugler's argument against this possibility that Jeremiah gives the impression of wishing to exclude the blood-covenant, i.e. the idea of sacrifice, and that this would not harmonize with the thought of Jesus concerning his death. Gaugler suggests that the obvious allusion to Jeremiah in 'new covenant' is due to Paul who, ignoring the rest of the meaning of covenant in the mind of that prophet, fixed on the single reminiscence 'new'.[4] Certainly, as Behm has rightly emphasized,[5] the Old Testament covenant conception is the basis of Paul's new theology of history. It may be added that the exact expression 'new covenant' ($\kappa\alpha\iota\nu\dot{\eta}\ \delta\iota\alpha\theta\dot{\eta}\kappa\eta$) is in any case Pauline; it occurs in 2 Cor. 3.6, where the allusion to Jer. 31.31 ff is mani-

---

[1] Op. cit., p. 99.
[2] Dalman, op. cit., pp. 160 f suggests as a literal Aramaic version of the Greek *idmi diḳeyāmā*, or better, *idmi deliḳeyāmā*, although the proper Aramaic would be *adam ḳeyāmi*, 'my blood-of-the-covenant', 'my covenant-blood'.
[3] J. Jeremias, op. cit., p. 99; G. Dalman, op. cit., p. 167.
[4] Op. cit., pp. 17, 40.
[5] In Kittel's *Theologisches Wörterbuch*, ii, 1935, p. 133.

fest: 'God, who has qualified us to be ministers of a new covenant, not in a written code, but in the Spirit.' The inference is that Paul himself is responsible for the form of the cup saying which identifies the cup with a new covenant.

We have, then, no evidence that at his last meal with his disciples Jesus spoke of a new covenant, or, indeed, that he spoke of a covenant at all.[1] This is not to deny that the *idea* of a new covenant as foretold by Jeremiah may have been present in his mind.

To sum up this comparison of the variant forms of the cup saying in Mark and Paul. The former represents the older strand of tradition, in which, however, the mention of the covenant is a subsequent, though very early addition. The Pauline version, in which the saying is remodelled to make the covenant idea central, is due to Paul's emphasis on the covenant, and to his representation of the Last Supper as the inauguration of a new covenant ratified in the blood of Christ. The matter is well put by W. D. Davies. 'In this Paul is making explicit what was implicit in the tradition that he had received. That Jesus had thought in terms of a New Covenant instituted through His Death we cannot doubt, and He may even have actually expounded His thought at the Last Supper to this effect.... In any case the concept of the New Covenant is only implicit.'[2]

(*c*) *The absence from Mark of the command to repeat*

> 1 Cor. 11.24. 'Do this in remembrance of me.'
> 1 Cor. 11.25 (after the cup). 'Do this, as often as you drink it, in remembrance of me.'

Here we are faced with the most remarkable difference between the two accounts. The absence from Mark of the double com-

---

[1] Cf. M. Dibelius, op. cit., p. 209: 'Hence, especially, the question cannot be answered whether Jesus spoke anything about the new "covenant" when dispensing the cup'.

[2] Op. cit., p. 251; cf. also J. Jeremias, op. cit., p. 99, n. 7, who does not wish to imply that the necessary omission of 'covenant' in the saying according to Mark involves the denial that Jesus thought that the new covenant of Jer. 31.31 ff was being realized.

The Eucharistic Sayings of Jesus: their Form

mand to repeat surely means that it was unknown to him, for otherwise it is hard to understand why he should have omitted it; perhaps it fell out of his branch of the tradition on the principle of P. Benoit's dictum, *On ne récite pas une rubrique, on l'exécute*.[1]

Does the injunction to repeat what was done at the Last Supper belong to a tradition utilized by Paul, or is it his own creation? The second alternative has been advanced, notably by Lietzmann, who suggested that it was the apostle who, in his emphasis on the death of Christ, transformed the Lord's Supper in his churches from a continuation of the fellowship meals enjoyed by the first disciples with their earthly Lord into a commemoration of his death. In this, according to Lietzmann, Paul was influenced by the contemporary Hellenistic practice of the holding of feasts in memory of the dead by relatives and friends on the anniversary of their death, or more frequently[2]; and the language of the formulae of the foundation of these memorial feasts often strongly resembles that of the command to repeat the Lord's Supper. The Lord's Supper in the New Testament, however, is in fact far more than a memorial feast. It possesses a strong eschatological outlook; and on his last night our Lord looked forward with confidence to a rendezvous with his friends in the Kingdom of God. Moreover, the Last Supper was in all probability a Passover meal, and therefore a firm feature of that festival may explain the injunction that the Last Supper was to be repeated as a remembrance.

The following key passages illustrate the centrality of the idea of remembrance in the Passover.

Ex. 12.14: 'And this day shall be unto you for a *memorial* (*lezikkaron*, LXX μνημόσυνον), and you shall keep it a feast to the Lord: throughout your generations you shall keep it a feast by an ordinance for ever.'

Deut. 16.3: 'That thou mayest *remember* the day when thou camest forth out of the land of Egypt all the days of thy life.'

---
[1] Cited by J. Jeremias, op. cit., p. 115.
[2] *Messe und Herrenmahl*, 1926, p. 223, and *An die Korinther I-II*, 4th edn., 1949, p. 58.

Ex. 13.3: '*Remember* this day, in which you came out from Egypt.'

Ex. 13.9: 'And it shall be for a sign unto thee upon thine hand, and for a *memorial* (*lezikkaron*, LXX μνημόσυνον) between thine eyes.'

The precept to tell the children the meaning of the festival (Ex. 12.26 f; 13.8) is the basis of the Passover Haggadah, by which the memory of the event is to be kept fresh, and each individual in every generation is to feel that he shares in the deliverance from Egypt.

It is held by W. D. Davies,[1] but from quite a different angle than that of Lietzmann, that the command to repeat 'in remembrance' is due to Paul, who, regarding the Last Supper as a new Passover, has imported into it the element of remembrance which is characteristic of the latter. One wonders, however, how Paul could have been the first to do this, though Davies, it is true, does allow that he was but making explicit what was already implicit, and even in the mind of Jesus himself.

Strongly in favour of the possibility that the words 'Do this in remembrance of me' should be attributed not to Paul, but to a tradition used by him is the un-Pauline language of the whole pericope.[2] But to say that they belong to a tradition is not necessarily to admit their authenticity, especially as they are missing from Mark. We cannot really be certain whether Jesus in so many words enjoined the repetition of what was done at the Last Supper, though the tradition that he did is certainly in harmony with his intention on that occasion.

The command to repeat after the bread is reported also by Luke. The repetition of the same command after the cup, in the form 'Do this, *as often as* you drink it, in remembrance of me' (not in Luke) should be attributed to Paul himself, especially in view of the immediately following remark of Paul, 'For *as often as* you eat this bread and drink the cup . . .'[3]

[1] Op. cit., p. 252.
[2] See above, p. 26.   [3] See above, p. 26, n.13.

The Eucharistic Sayings of Jesus: their Form

(*d*) *The absence from the Pauline version of the eschatological saying in Mark 14.25*

>Mark 14.25. 'Verily I say unto you, that I shall not drink again of the fruit of the vine until that day when I drink it new in the Kingdom of God.'

Although Paul does not record this saying of Jesus, 1 Cor. 11.26 ('For as often as you eat this bread and drink the cup you proclaim the Lord's death until he comes') shows that his tradition of the Last Supper preserved the eschatological thought enshrined in it. As in Mark the eschatological utterance follows immediately the saying at the dispensing of the cup, so Paul's reminder that participation in the Lord's Supper is a proclamation of the Lord's death 'until he comes' follows the distribution of the cup by Jesus and his command to drink in memory of him. Luke (22.18) reports this eschatological saying in a less Semitic and therefore less original form than Mark,[1] but probably, as we shall see, more correctly places it at the beginning of the meal instead of at the end.

We turn now to the rather complex question of the Last Supper in Luke.

3. *The Last Supper in Luke*

>Luke 22.15-20. (15) And he said to them, I have earnestly desired to eat this Passover with you before I suffer; (16) for I say to you that I shall not eat it until it is fulfilled in the Kingdom of God. (17) And he took a cup and gave thanks and said, Take this, and divide it among yourselves; (18) for I say to you that henceforth I shall not drink of the fruit of the vine until the Kingdom of God comes. (19*a*) And he took bread and gave thanks and broke it, and gave to them saying, This is my body [(19*b*) which is given for you; do this in remembrance of me. (20) And the cup likewise after supper, saying, This cup is the new covenant in my blood, and it is poured out for you].

The text as given above is the so-called 'longer text' which is read by all Greek manuscripts except D, and by most of the

---
[1] See J. Jeremias, op. cit., pp. 87 f.

versions except some of the Old Latin authorities and the Old Syriac.

The 'shorter text', which omits verses 19*b* and 20 (enclosed in square brackets), is the text of the Western manuscript D and of certain Old Latin manuscripts (a, d, ff², i, l).

Two of the more important Old Latin manuscripts (b and e) arrange the verses in the order: 15, 16, 19*a*, 17, 18. They support the witnesses to the shorter text, because the object of the transposition is to restore the usual order bread–cup, and this would have been unnecessary had the longer form of text been known to those responsible for the readjustment. The Old Syriac version's similar rearrangement of verses probably represents an independent attempt to do the same thing.

This means that the shorter text was at an early date to be found in western Europe (D and its supporting Old Latin witnesses), in Africa (e), and in Syria.

Both the longer and the shorter texts are peculiar when compared with the Markan and Pauline accounts of the Last Supper.

The shorter text is peculiar in its order cup—bread. The same order is, indeed, found in 1 Cor. 10.16, 21, but this signifies nothing, since Paul in his account of the Last Supper follows the normal order. It has also been claimed that the so-called evidence supplied by Luke for a Eucharist with the elements in the reverse of the usual order is supported by that of the *Didache* 9 ('First, as regards the cup: We give thee thanks; ... then as regards the broken bread: We give thee thanks'). It seems more probable, however, as Jeremias argues,[1] that in 9, 10.1-5 we have to do with the *agape* or common fellowship meal which is followed by the Eucharist proper, for the words in 10.6 ('If any is holy, let him come; if any is not, let him repent. *Marana tha* (Our Lord, come)') really only fit the introduction of a Eucharist,[2] and not its conclusion. There is, therefore, no evidence here for the order cup—bread; and in the *Didache* 14 the weekly Eucharist is described as the breaking of bread and the giving of thanks, with no details

---

[1] Op. cit., p. 66.   [2] Cf. also R. Bultmann, op. cit., p. 149.

The Eucharistic Sayings of Jesus: their Form

as to the order of distribution of the elements. No more is the shorter text of Luke really evidence of an anomalous order in eucharistic practice. As we shall see, the cup in verse 17 is not a eucharistic cup. A second peculiarity of the shorter Lukan text is its abrupt ending with the words 'This is my body'. Champions of this text as the more original suppose verses 19*b* and 20 to have been added to restore the order bread—cup in accordance with prevalent liturgical usage. The difficulty is that the result of this addition is the production of two cups, whereas liturgical practice knew only one cup.

The peculiar feature of the longer text is the presence of these two cups. The supporters of the originality of this text suppose the shorter text to be an abbreviation designed to remove one of these cups. But it is strange that, if this was the case, it was not the *first* cup which was removed,[1] because this is so different from the eucharistic cup in Mark and Paul. Moreover, the resultant shorter text destroys the normal order of the elements.

Now the overwhelming weight of manuscript authority is on the side of the longer text. Why should it have been shortened? Clearly the usual explanation is somewhat inadequate. Two alternative solutions have been offered.

According to the former of these, verses 19*b* and 20 were omitted in certain circles in order to preserve the *arcanum* or esoteric secret of the sacred rite, just as in Hellenistic custom the actual words of the mysteries must not be divulged except to initiates.[2] The objection to this explanation of the genesis of the short text is that one would surely have expected 'this is my body' also to be omitted as part of the secret.[3]

---

[1] As in the Peshitta Syriac, which omits verses 17 and 18.
[2] Cf. G. D. Kilpatrick in *Journal of Theological Studies*, xlvii, 1946, pp. 52 ff; J. Jeremias, op. cit., pp. 59, 79. Jeremias (p. 59) also mentions the Essenes as observing an analogous practice in Palestine in New Testament times. G. Dalman, op. cit., p. 156, suggests the possibility of the words concerning the wine having been suppressed, 'since they might be misunderstood, and lead to accusations against Christ's followers'.
[3] This *disciplina arcani* theory is rejected by E. Lohmeyer in *Theologische Rundschau*, ix, 1937, pp. 300, 291 (the principle of the preservation of the *arcanum* operates from the third century onwards, not in primitive Christianity), and by E. Gaugler, op. cit.,.p 20.

The second alternative is to strike out verse 19*a* in addition to 19*b* and 20,[1] so as to make the shorter text comprise verses 15-18 only. This solution is untenable because there is no textual evidence to support it.

Another way must be found. The predominant manuscript authority in favour of the longer text and the difficulty of accounting for its awkward and abrupt abbreviation by the omission of verses 19*b* and 20 point in the same direction. I would suggest that the text of Luke as we have it now is the original one, and that it is a combination by the evangelist of two traditions, the one consisting of verses 15-19*a*, and the other of verses 19*a*-20. Luke (and those who left his account of the Last Supper unchanged) felt no difficulty in the presence of the two cups, because the first was not regarded as a eucharistic cup. The omission of verses 19*b*-20 is the work of circles which knew a tradition of the Last Supper similar in form to that utilized by the evangelist in verses 15-19*a*, while those who were responsible for the change in the sequence of verses to 15, 16, 19*a*, 17, 18 were not satisfied with the anomalous order cup—bread in the shorter text as it came to them. Common to both traditions is verse 19*a*, 'And he took bread and gave thanks and broke it, and gave to them saying, This is my body'. This is because the words are the central and essential feature both of the Last Supper of our Lord, which is the primary, though not the sole concern of the tradition embodied in verses 15-19*a*, and of the Church's Eucharist which strongly colours the form of the narrative in verses 19*a*-20.

What is the value of verses 15-18? Do they, as suggested, represent part of an independent tradition adopted by Luke, or are they, as Lietzmann[2] supposed, a purely literary construction of the third evangelist, who has transferred to the beginning of the meal Mark's eschatological saying following the saying over

---

[1] K. L. Schmidt (who also removes verse 17), 'Abendmahl im Neuen Testament' in *Die Religion in Geschichte und Gegenwart*, 2nd edn., i, 1927, cols. 7-10; H. N. Bate, 'The "Shorter Text" of St Luke XXII 15-20' in *Journal of Theological Studies*, xxviii, 1927, pp. 367 f; R. Bultmann, *Die Geschichte der synoptischen Tradition*, 2nd edn., 1931, p. 286, n. 1.

[2] *Messe und Herrenmahl*, 1926, pp. 216 f.

The Eucharistic Sayings of Jesus: their Form

the wine, and has prefixed a parallel eschatological saying referring to the (Passover) meal as a whole?

Let us first consider verse 18, 'For I say to you that henceforth I shall not drink of the fruit of the vine until the Kingdom of God comes'. There is no reason to question the substantial authenticity of this utterance, which is recorded also in Mark 14.25 in a variant form. Indeed Goguel, who regards it as genuine[1] and similar to other sayings of Jesus which compare the Kingdom of God to a banquet, even judges that it is the source not only of Luke 22.16, which was created as a parallel to it, but also of the (to him) secondary covenant-cup saying.[2] Does it come more appropriately at the conclusion of the meal, as in Mark, or at the beginning, as in Luke? The majority of critics seem to prefer the Lukan position, where the connection with what precedes is certainly more satisfactory than in Mark, whose order has the additional disadvantage that in the word of institution the wine is compared to covenant blood which is to be shed sacrificially, while in the next sentence it is called 'the fruit of the vine', and is mentioned in order to centre the thoughts of the disciples on the renewal of fellowship in the Kingdom of God. Moreover, in the blessing over the first Passover cup the wine was called 'the fruit of the vine',[3] so that it has been thought that this is the cup referred to in Luke 22.17 f.[4] It is unlikely that the position of the saying in

---

[1] Op. cit., p. 83.
[2] Id., pp. 81, 87 f, 288, and *L'église primitive*, 1947, p. 345. It is, perhaps, worth noting that to Loisy (*Les évangiles synoptiques*, ii, 1908, p. 539) the words 'This is my body' were also secondary, and arose from Luke 22.16, which in its original form expressed Jesus' refusal to eat *bread* until the advent of the Kingdom.
[3] Mishnah, *Berakoth* 6.1.
[4] E. Schweizer, in an important article entitled 'Das Abendmahl eine Vergegenwärtigung des Todes Jesu oder ein eschatologisches Freudenmahl?' in *Theologische Zeitschrift*, ii, 2 (March-April 1946), argues tentatively (pp. 96-98), following H. J. Holtzmann (*Die Synoptiker*, 1901, p. 409), for the opposite view, on the grounds that Mark is otherwise the more reliable witness, and likely to be so with the eschatological utterance; that eschatological-Messianic joy at the Passover is at least as well attested in connection with the third cup, after the meal, as with the first cup; that the former was the more important because of the prayers spoken over it; and that in the time of Jesus the third cup was followed by the singing of the latter part of the Hallel, which expressed eschatological expectations characteristic of the Passover. In short, according to Schweizer, the only thing in favour of Luke's placing of this saying is the phrase 'the fruit of the vine'.

Luke is due to the evangelist's having transferred it from its place in Mark, because, as is well known, Luke dislikes transposing Mark's order of events.[1] The answer to the difficulty probably is that the eschatological saying occupied different places in the special tradition here followed by Luke and in the Markan tradition. We conclude that the Lukan order is the correct one, but that Mark preserves the more original form of the saying.[2]

In answer to the contention that Luke 22.16 ('For I say to you that I shall not eat it until it is fulfilled in the Kingdom of God') is a creation of the evangelist to balance verse 18, it has been pointed out that this again is contrary to the method of Luke, who, so far from producing parallelisms, tends to remove them where he finds them in his sources.[3] If it is urged against this first eschatological utterance in Luke that Mark, who has only the second, referring to wine, is not likely to have shortened an original double saying,[4] the reply is that the first one is absent from Mark because it was unknown to him. While it formed part of Luke's special source, but not that of Mark, 'the first eschatological saying in verse 16 is no mere redundant variation of the second in verse 18'.[5]

We must reckon with the strong probability that Luke 22.15-18 (or rather 15-19a) represents a tradition of considerable value.[6] It is not being suggested that the evangelist has not to some extent been responsible for the form in which he presents the tradition. In this tradition of the Last Supper which, like the Markan-Pauline version, is possibly influenced by eucharistic usage as practised in certain circles (but to a far lesser degree), nothing is said of the eucharistic cup after the bread. This silence does not

---

[1] Cf. J. Jeremias, op. cit., pp. 56, 87.
[2] Cf. F. J. Leenhardt, op. cit., p. 41, n. 1, who remarks that the value of Luke's source is not affected by the verbal changes he has introduced.
[3] Cf. J. Jeremias, op. cit., p. 87.
[4] Cf. E. Schweizer, op. cit., p. 97.
[5] G. H. C. Macgregor, *Eucharistic Origins*, 1928, p. 62.
[6] Cf. e.g. J. Behm, art. κλάω in Kittel's *Theologisches Wörterbuch zum Neuen Testament*, iii, 1938, p. 731. M. Goguel, *L'église primitive*, 1947, p. 344 writes: 'Des trois récits du dernier repas du Nouveau Testament c'est celui de Luc qui paraît représenter le plus exactement ce qui s'est passé.'

The Eucharistic Sayings of Jesus: their Form

necessarily imply that Luke 22.15-19a points to a *communio sub una*. The primary value of this tradition is that it supplements our other information of what transpired at the Last Supper.

We turn to verses 19a-20.

It is an axiom of modern study of the Synoptic Gospels that Luke used Mark as one of his main sources. He therefore presumably knew Mark's account of the Last Supper. Further, as a companion of Paul, he was surely acquainted with the eucharistic practice of the Pauline churches, even if he did not actually know 1 Cor. 11.23-25. At first sight Luke 22.19-20 looks like a mere combination of material borrowed from Mark and Paul, and is often regarded as that and nothing more. In order to bring out the striking resemblances of Luke both to Mark and Paul, the three accounts are given below, with the elements common to Luke and Mark in capitals, and those common to Luke and Paul in italics.

Luke 22.19-20

(19) And he took bread and gave thanks and broke it, AND GAVE TO THEM saying, This is my body *which is given for you; do this in remembrance of me.* (20) *And the cup likewise after supper, saying, This cup is the new covenant in my blood*, and it IS POURED OUT FOR you.

Mark 14.22-24

(22) He took bread and blessed, and broke it, AND GAVE TO THEM, and said, Take; this is my body. (23) And he took a cup, and when he had given thanks he gave it to them, and they all drank of it. (24) And he said to them, This is my blood of the covenant which IS POURED OUT FOR many.

1 *Cor.* 11.23-25

(23) (The Lord Jesus) . . . took bread, (24) and when he had given thanks he broke it, and said, This is my body *which is for you. Do this in remembrance of me.* (25) *Likewise also the cup after*

supper, saying, This cup is the new covenant in my blood. Do this, as often as you drink it, in remembrance of me.[1]

Reasons have already been advanced for the belief that Paul's form of the saying over the cup is his own,[2] and that the second command to repeat is to be attributed to him, while the first was in his tradition.[3] It does not seem likely that Luke has used Paul's account of the Last Supper, for otherwise one would have expected the inclusion of the second command to repeat as well as the first, especially as the desire for balance of expression, as evidenced in the corresponding phrases 'given for you' and 'poured out for you' would have been further satisfied. Neither are the contacts between Luke and Mark here necessarily due to Luke's direct use of Mark. It may rather be that Luke 22.19-20 is independent evidence of the same tradition as that used by Paul, a tradition which included a command to repeat after the bread but not after the cup; and that this tradition, by the time it came to Luke, had been influenced by another such as is embodied in Mark, and had incorporated a new formulation of the cup saying which originated with the interpretative genius of Paul.

[1] There are some trifling variations of Luke from Paul in what is common to them. Luke has ὡσαύτως after ποτήριον, omits ἐστίν, and for ἐμῷ αἵματι has αἵματί μου to balance σῶμά μου (τοῦτό ἐστι τὸ σῶμά μου as in Mark). More important is Luke's addition of διδόμενον to τὸ ὑπὲρ ὑμῶν (Paul), which exactly balances τὸ ὑπὲρ ὑμῶν ἐκχυννόμενον (=Mark, except for πολλῶν). This latter phrase is most awkward because 'blood', to which ἐκχυννόμενον refers, is in the dative. In Mark all is well, because αἷμα is nominative. Jeremias (op. cit., p. 77) thinks this awkward grammar would not be felt in liturgy, and is actually a sign of liturgical use.
[2] See above, pp. 31, 33 f.
[3] See above, p. 36.

CHAPTER FOUR

THE EUCHARISTIC SAYINGS OF JESUS: THEIR MEANING

In this chapter we shall be concerned with the interpretation of the words of Jesus at the Last Supper whose original form and extent we have tried to recover. As a preliminary to this task it will be useful to place them in their paschal context, on the assumption that the Last Supper was very probably a Passover meal.

Passover[1]

1. *Hors d'oeuvre.* The head of the household over the first cup pronounces the blessing for the day and a blessing for the wine, which is then drunk by him and the others present. The first blessing is the *kiddush*, the second would have been in the traditional form, 'Blessed art thou who createst the fruit of the vine'.[2] Then are eaten green herbs, bitter herbs, and *haroseth*, a sauce consisting of fruits, spices, and vinegar into which the bitter herbs are dipped.

Last Supper

Luke 22.15. And he said to them, *I have earnestly desired to eat this Passover with you before I suffer;* (16) *for I say to you that I shall not eat it until it is fulfilled in the Kingdom of God.*

Luke 22.17. And he took a cup and gave thanks and said, *Take this, and divide it among yourselves;* (18) *for I say to you that henceforth I shall not drink of the fruit of the vine until the Kingdom of God comes* (=Mark 14.25. *Verily I say unto you, that I shall not drink again of the fruit of the vine until that day when I drink it new in the Kingdom of God*).

---

[1] For the probable order of observance in the time of Jesus the chief authorities are: Strack-Billerbeck, *Kommentar zum Neuen Testament aus Talmud und Midrasch*, iv, 1928, pp. 41-76; J. Behm, art. κλάω in G. Kittel's *Theologisches Wörterbuch zum Neuen Testament*, iii, 1938, pp. 732 f; J. Jeremias, *Die Abendmahlsworte Jesu*, 2nd edn., 1949, pp. 47-49; cf. G. Dalman, *Jesus-Jeshua*, Eng. tr., 1929, pp. 106 ff.

[2] Mishnah, *Berakoth* 6.1. This is the order observed by the school of Shammai The rival school of Hillel reversed the order of the blessings, Mishnah, *Pesahim* 10.2

The Lord's Supper in the New Testament

2. *Haggadah.* When the food (unleavened bread, the roast lamb, wine, bitter herbs, etc.) for the meal proper is brought in, the son in a household asks his father why this night differs from other nights in several respects, particularly in that all the bread is unleavened. The reply is that the Passover lamb is eaten 'because God passed over the houses of our fathers in Egypt' (Ex. 12.26 f); unleavened bread 'because our fathers were redeemed from Egypt' (cf. Ex. 12.39); bitter herbs 'because the Egyptians embittered the lives of our fathers in Egypt' (cf. Ex. 1.14). Everyone must regard himself as if *he* had come out of Egypt (cf. Ex. 13.8).[1]

Jesus' description of himself as the true Passover lamb.

3. The singing of the first part of the Hallel (according to the school of Shammai, Ps. 113; according to the school of Hillel, Pss. 113 and 114).

4. The drinking of a second cup of wine.

5. The president takes unleavened bread, blesses God in the words, 'Blessed art thou who bringest forth bread from the earth', and breaks it in pieces which he hands to the guests.

Mark 14.22. ... He took bread and blessed, and broke it, and gave to them, and said, *Take; this is my body.* (1 Cor. 11.24; Luke 22.19. *Do this in remembrance of me.*)

6. The meal proper.

7. At the conclusion the president offers a prayer of thanksgiving for the meal over a third cup, 'the cup of blessing' (cf. 1 Cor. 10.16).

Mark 14.23. And he took a cup (Likewise also the cup after supper, 1 Cor. 11.25; Luke 22.20), and when he had given thanks he gave it to them, and they all drank of it. (24) And he said to them, *This is my blood, which is poured out for many.*

[1] Mishnah, *Pesahim* 10.4, 5.

The Eucharistic Sayings of Jesus: their Meaning

8. The singing of the second part of the Hallel.   Mark 14.26. And when they had sung a hymn, they went out to the Mount of Olives.

We shall take these sayings of Jesus in the following order:
1. Luke 22.15-18; Mark 14.25
2. Mark 14.22; 14.24
3. 1 Cor. 11.24; Luke 22.19.

1. *Luke 22.15-18; Mark 14.25*

Luke in verse 15 is clearly concerned to stress the paschal character of the Last Supper. Yet it does not necessarily follow that this verse is not based on an authentic utterance of Jesus expressing his eager desire to share this last meal with his disciples, although the language of the Church has reacted on its form. The word 'suffer' without any object may well be due to this cause. Before the meal begins Jesus declares that he knows his end is so near that this is bound to be the last earthly Passover for him. Similarly, as recorded both by Luke and Mark, he announces (when dispensing the first cup, according to the former) that this is the last occasion on which he will be able to taste wine. But the emphasis is not on the sorrow of parting, but on the joyful expectation of the renewal of fellowship in the Kingdom of God. When he meets his friends again, the Passover will have been transcended by the Messianic banquet in the Kingdom.

This joyful eschatological outlook is by no means an importation by Jesus into the Passover celebration. It is an integral part of the Jewish feast. It was said that Passover night was a time of joy for all Israel.[1] At the Passover the deliverance from Egypt is the prefiguration of the even greater redemption to come. Thus it was said by Joshua ben Hananiah (c. A.D. 90) that Passover night was the night on which the Jews had been redeemed in the past, and on which they will be redeemed in the future.[2] Of the month of Nisan in which Passover fell it was said: 'The Messiah, who is called the first (Isa. 41.27), will come in the first month'.[3]

---

[1] *Exodus Rabbah* 18.11.   [2] *Mekhilta* Ex. 12.42.   [3] *Exodus Rabbah* 15.1.

Elijah was expected on the Passover day.[1] Beliefs of this kind tend to be expanded by the addition of further details, and so we hear of a later practice of setting a place for Elijah as the forerunner of the Messiah.[2] Much more of the kind could be adduced to show that the element of expectant joy was ingrained in the Passover.

As G. Dalman[3] says, the Kingdom of God 'is itself fundamentally the fulfilment of the Passover, as it brings into fruition, in the most perfect measure, and finally, the transition from bondage to freedom, and the consummation of the people of God'. When Jesus spoke of the Kingdom in this way on his last night, he was repeating that comparison of the Kingdom with a banquet which was often on his lips (Luke 13.29; Matt. 8.11; 22.1 ff; Luke 22.30). And in so referring to the Kingdom he was using language readily understood by his hearers and familiar to them. There is a striking analogy in 1 *Enoch* 62.14:

> 'And the Lord of Spirits will abide over them,
> And with that Son of Man shall they eat
> And lie down and rise up for ever and ever.'[4]

It is, therefore, certainly right to lay due emphasis on the joyful aspect of the Eucharist. Jesus looked forward, and would have his disciples look forward to the greater banquet of the Kingdom of God, when all the Passover promises of eschatological joy, of redemption, and of the glorious Messianic age should be fulfilled. Luke 22.15-18 makes this much clearer than Mark, while the predominant use of Paul's interpretation of the Lord's Supper as primarily a memorial feast has tended to push it into the background. At the same time, it is equally mistaken to lay all the emphasis upon this eschatological element. The classic example

---

[1] *Exodus Rabbah* 18.12.
[2] Cf. the modern 'cup of Elijah', a spare cup which is brought out but not used, A. A. Green, *The Revised Hagada*, 1897, p. 20. Cf. G. F. Moore, *Judaism*, ii, 1927, p. 42.
[3] Op. cit., p. 130.
[4] Other passages are cited by A. Schweitzer, *The Mysticism of Paul the Apostle*, Eng. tr., 1931, pp. 237 f. We are reminded of Rev. 19.9, 'Blessed are they who have been invited to the marriage supper of the Lamb'.

The Eucharistic Sayings of Jesus: their Meaning

of this is A. Schweitzer who, in what may be taken as a typical expression of his views on this question, writes: 'What constitutes the essential character of the Early Christian meal is [therefore] not a reference to Jesus' saying about the bread and wine as His body and blood, but *wholly and solely* in the petition and thanksgiving for the Coming of the Kingdom'.[1]

2. Mark 14.22. *'Take; this is my body.'*[2]

Mark 14.24. *'This is my blood which is poured out for many.'*

The disciples must have regarded these words, spoken by Jesus at the dispensing of the unleavened bread and of the third cup, as an astonishing addition to the customary observance; and their astonishment would have been greater still had their minds not been prepared for them by any previous explanation. What seems sudden and unexplained as, for example, the call of the disciples, must have been preceded by other incidents of which the Gospels, which are masterpieces of brevity and understatement, tell us nothing. If the Last Supper was a Passover meal, the words over the bread and the wine were suggested by the presence of the lamb on the table before the guests. The idea that Jesus (and not only the early Church, in the Fourth Gospel, 1 Cor. 5.7, 1 Peter 1.19, and Rev. 5.6) regarded himself as the true Passover lamb is, of course, not new.[3] In what sense, however, can he have compared himself with the paschal lamb? On the answer to this

---

[1] Op. cit., p. 251. The italics are mine.

[2] The Aramaic for 'my body' would be *guphi* (G. Dalman, op. cit., p. 143). Jeremias (op. cit., pp. 103 f), however, opposes this on the ground that the true complement to 'blood' is *flesh*; σῶμα, as well as σάρξ, can represent the Hebrew word for 'flesh' (*basar*), as it does a number of times in the Septuagint; what Jesus said was 'This is my *flesh*' (Aramaic *bisri*). This possibility does not affect the interpretation of the words of institution here suggested. K. G. Goetz (*Das Abendmahl eine Diatheke Jesu oder sein letztes Gleichnis?* 1920, pp. 62-65) also thinks Jesus spoke of his *flesh*, and the words mean 'I (my flesh and my blood) am food and drink'. Jeremias further believes that John 6.51-56, 63 and the epistles of Ignatius, in which σάρξ is used instead of σῶμα, represent a branch of tradition of the eucharistic words of Jesus according to which he spoke not of his body, but of his flesh. This also is possible, although the prevalent view is that the Fourth Gospel deliberately made the change from 'body' to 'flesh' for theological reasons. See further below, pp. 82 f.

[3] Among the exponents of this view may be mentioned R. H. Kennett, *The Last Supper, its Significance in the Upper Room*, 1921, p. 38, who, however, held that the Last Supper was an ordinary meal held twenty-four hours before the Passover.

question depends the interpretation of the two words of institution.

The most natural place for Jesus to have drawn the comparison would have been during the Passover Haggadah, which included an explanation of the meaning of the Passover lamb.[1] This Haggadah was based on the narrative in Ex. 12, according to which the Passover lambs slain at the time of the Exodus were a sacrifice, the sprinkling of whose blood on the lintel and door posts had the result that the Lord spared the first-born sons of the Israelites 'and delivered our houses'. There is no need to argue the point that Jesus attached a sacrificial and redemptive significance to his death. We have only to point to Mark 10.45, 'The Son of Man came not to be served, but to serve, and to give his life a ransom for many'. Neither is there any doubt that in referring to his body and blood he was at his last meal thinking of his imminent death as a sacrifice; his blood is to be 'poured out for many'. But was the paschal victim, with which Jesus compared himself, regarded as an atoning sacrifice which removed sin? It is clear that it was not. 'The Paschal victim was not a sin-offering or regarded as a means of expiating or removing sins.'[2] On the other hand, certain evidence might be held to support the belief that this was not the case with the lambs slain at the actual Exodus.[3] Whether this is so or not, it is not necessary to suppose that Jesus confined his thought to the current interpretation of the Passover, assuming that this in his day possessed no atoning significance, and that he could not have compared himself with the paschal lamb in the absence of this significance.

I would venture the suggestion that at the Last Supper our

---

[1] J. Jeremias, op. cit., p. 105.

[2] G. B. Gray, *Sacrifice in the Old Testament*, 1925, p. 397. Cf. also G. Dalman, op. cit., pp. 122 f, who lays the emphasis on the killing and eating of the lamb as a remembrance of redemption from slavery in Egypt, and who denies that Jesus saw in the Passover lamb a symbol of his death. He adds (p. 126): 'Anyone who has ever seen the Samaritans sit round the dish, ravenously munching their Passover meat, understands how impossible it would have been to connect words meant to refer to a higher archetype of the Passover lamb, with the formless remnants of a sheep, surrounded by people thus eager to consume it.'

[3] J. Jeremias, op. cit., pp. 107 f.

The Eucharistic Sayings of Jesus: their Meaning

Lord may have combined two different conceptions, as in the case of the Son of Man and the Servant of the Lord. The name for the paschal victim was the Passover, and this could be not only a sheep or lamb, but also a goat.[1] While the lamb was probably the commoner in the time of Jesus, the permitted use of a goat as the paschal victim would have suggested the great Day of Atonement ritual (Lev. 16), in which one of the two goats was killed as a sin-offering, and the other, after the performance over it of some rite of atonement, bore 'upon him all their iniquities to a solitary land'. The First Epistle of Peter associates the Passover lamb and the scapegoat in describing the atoning work of Christ,[2] and it is possible that the association originated with Jesus, though it may remain doubtful whether perhaps the goat sacrificed as a sin-offering was uppermost in his mind, rather than the scapegoat itself.

The upshot is that Jesus at the Last Supper alluded to his approaching death as a sacrifice of atoning efficacy, and likened himself to the Passover lamb whose death had already taken place.

We now turn to the actual words spoken by Jesus in connection with the bread and wine. The interpretations of these words are legion, which it is no part of our purpose to review. But it is necessary to clear the ground by removing two widespread but erroneous opinions. The first is the Catholic view that 'is' ($\dot{\epsilon}\sigma\tau\iota$) must be taken literally—the bread and wine are in fact, if not in appearance, the actual body and blood of Christ. Such a belief would have been quite impossible to a Jew. The word 'is', which would not be expressed in Aramaic, must signify 'means', 'represents', or 'stands for'. The second is the popular idea that the *tertium comparationis* is, in the case of the bread, its breaking, in that of the wine, the pouring out, representing the violent death of Jesus, and the shedding of his blood. This cannot be so, for the first word of institution was said not at the breaking of the bread, but at its distribution. It was, besides, customary in Palestine to break the bread with the hands at any meal, and there is

---

[1] Ex. 12.5; see G. B. Gray, op. cit., pp. 344 ff.
[2] E. G. Selwyn, *The First Epistle of St. Peter*, 1946, pp. 94 f; *per contra* F. W. Beare, *The First Epistle of Peter*, 1947, p. 123.

therefore no significance in its mention here. The same applies to the wine, which was poured from the mixing bowl into the cup before it was offered by Jesus to the disciples.

It is easy to understand that Jesus should have used the red wine of the Passover to represent his blood, for in the Old Testament wine is called the blood of the grape (Gen. 49.11; Deut. 32.14; cf. Rev. 14.20). It is not so easy to see why he should have chosen the bread as the symbol of his body. He could not use the lamb, for the eating of its flesh was from time immemorial a remembrance of the deliverance from Egypt. Moreover, to have chosen the flesh of the lamb to represent his body and to have distributed it in this sense would have involved a certain crudity which would have been repulsive to a Jew. To have compared himself with the paschal lamb in the Passover Haggadah is quite a different matter from this. Jesus invested the wine of the third Passover cup, which concluded the meal proper, with a new and unparalleled significance by associating it with his blood about to be shed. Similarly, he imparted an unprecedented meaning to the unleavened bread which opened the central part of the Passover meal. It was eaten 'because our fathers were redeemed from Egypt'; henceforth it would represent his body, soon to die. In other words, the two sayings 'This is my body' and 'This is my blood which is poured out for many' are interpolations into the Passover ritual at two vital points, before and after the main meal, whose central constituent is the flesh of the slain lamb, the Passover. Jesus tells the disciples that on this occasion and henceforth before eating the Passover they are to remember that the original meaning of the feast has been transcended. He is the fulfilment of the Passover victim; the customary unleavened bread now stands as a symbol of his body, the wine of 'the cup of blessing' as a symbol of his blood.

The disciples at the Last Supper are not to be regarded as eating (symbolically) the flesh of Christ in partaking of the bread, and as drinking his blood in taking the wine, but as remembering his sacrificial act. The real significance of the Passover lambs was

The Eucharistic Sayings of Jesus: their Meaning

that they *represented* the efficacious death of the lambs in Egypt—whether they were regarded as having effected atonement or solely deliverance of the Israelite households from the destroyer—but they possessed no efficacy themselves. In the same way the bread and wine of the Eucharist *represent* the atoning sacrifice of Christ as the true paschal lamb without themselves possessing any inherent efficacy. The Last Supper was the pattern of future celebrations of the Passover for the followers of Jesus. At the same time it was the prototype of the Eucharist. The experience and remembrance of all subsequent participants in the Eucharist was to the disciples 'in the night on which he was betrayed' proleptic and anticipatory, for the sacrifice they were to remember was still in the future. Both at the Passover and at the Eucharist the sacrificial death is presupposed and is no part of the actual meal. The Eucharist is therefore a proclamation and a remembrance of what has taken place—or, rather, of what God has done—just like the Passover. What is to be emphasized is not the eucharistic elements themselves, but the sacrificial act they call to mind.

This has rightly been recognized by two recent writers. M. Barth[1] remarks that the words of institution concern not the substance of the elements, but their use, and finds a close parallel to the word of Jesus concerning the bread in an old Aramaic formula based on Deut. 16.3, which runs: 'Behold, this is the bread of affliction which our fathers ate when they came out of Egypt.'[2] The Eucharist, therefore, is not a Passion play like the Mass[3]; Christ's death is preached (1 Cor. 11.26), not his dying re-enacted.[4] E. Gaugler[5] also emphasizes that the body and blood are not to be understood in a material sense, but as representative symbols of the *event* of Christ's death.

Since the bread and wine signify Christ's act of sacrifice, to be

---

[1] *Das Abendmahl: Passamahl, Bundesmahl, und Messiasmahl*, 1945, pp. 17, 19.
[2] See also G. Dalman, op. cit., p. 139 and J. Jeremias, op. cit., p. 31. This formula, however, was not spoken, like the word of Jesus, at the distribution of the bread, but formed part of the Haggadah, as it still does (see A. A. Green, op. cit., pp. 24 f); it is doubtful whether it was in use as early as the time of Jesus.
[3] M. Barth, op. cit., p. 28.   [4] Id., p. 30.
[5] *Das Abendmahl im Neuen Testament*, 1943, p. 45.

invited to partake of them as standing for his body and blood means to be bidden to be at one with him in his sacrifice, and so to share by anticipation in the fruits of his Passion in the Messianic meal in the Kingdom of God, the fulfilment of the Passover. Meanwhile the disciples will as Jews continue to observe the Passover, but it will be in remembrance of the salvation wrought through *him*; and in so doing they will know his spiritual presence. But the effect of the resurrection was that this commemoration was held every week: the weekly Lord's Supper replaced the Passover, and the lamb ceased to play any part, its central position being taken by the bread and the wine to which Jesus had attached a new and vital meaning. Thus the Church's Eucharist is at one and the same time a remembrance of the death of Christ, and an expectation of perfect joy with him in the Kingdom, which is already in a measure anticipated at each celebration by the experience of his risen living presence. There is no doubt that too often the first element, which is certainly absolutely fundamental to the Eucharist, has been allowed to exclude the other two, and that the modern Church has largely lost that forward-looking expectancy and eschatological joy and hope which were characteristic of the early communities. It is therefore necessary to protest when M. Barth,[1] who holds that at the Last Supper Jesus believed the advent of the Kingdom to be imminent, within a few days, declares that the promised Messianic meal in the Kingdom of God was fulfilled in the post-resurrection meals in Luke, Acts, and John (see Acts 10.41), and that therefore the Eucharist is the Messianic meal. This indefensible view involves the equation of the Church with the Kingdom of God, and implies that nothing remains for the future, since all is fulfilled already.[2]

[1] Op. cit., pp. 39 ff.
[2] Cf. V. Taylor, *Jesus and His Sacrifice*, 1943 (=1937), p. 185, n. 2, and for a criticism of Barth's position see E. Schweizer, 'Das Abendmahl eine Vergegenwärtigung des Todes Jesu oder ein eschatologisches Freudenmahl?' in *Theologische Zeitschrift*, ii, 2 (March-April 1946), p. 95, n. 78. The second-century *Epistle of the Apostles* (15) emphasizes the belief that the fulfilment of the Passover is still in the future after the resurrection has taken place, and that the Eucharist must be repeated until then; see the Eng. tr. in M. R. James, *The Apocryphal New Testament*, 1945 (=1924), p. 490.

The Eucharistic Sayings of Jesus: their Meaning

3. 1 Cor. 11.24; Luke 22.19. *'Do this in remembrance of me.'*

This command to repeat belongs to a tradition, but its omission from Mark gives rise to doubts about its authenticity. Yet it is in harmony with the intention of Jesus. The words will refer not only to the bread at whose distribution they are reported to have been uttered, but to the whole meal which followed. They express the wish of Jesus that the annual Passover should be observed in his memory[1] until the rendezvous in the Kingdom. The fact that the Church came to remember the Lord at the weekly breaking of bread and not at an annual Passover[2] should not be brought against the strong probability that what Jesus expected to happen was the latter. Similarly, Jesus expected soon to return in glory as the Son of Man at the Parousia, an expectation which was not fulfilled. The New Testament Church is the historical fulfilment of his new community, the true Israel within Israel; its weekly Eucharist is the historical counterpart to the new series of annual Passovers which in the expectation of Jesus were to differ from all previous ones in being centred upon him. But none can assert, whatever may be said of subsequent developments or aberrations, that the post-resurrection New Testament Church, with its Lord's Supper in remembrance of the sacrifice of Christ and in keen expectation of his return, would not have won the approval of the Lord had he been able to foresee it.

[1] Jeremias' interpretation of the words as meaning 'that *God* may remember me' by bringing in the Kingdom at the Parousia (op. cit., pp. 115-118) has been proved untenable by W. C. van Unnik, 'Kanttekeningen bij een nieuwe verklaring van de Anamnese-woorden' in *Nederlands Theologisch Tijdschrift*, iv, 6 (Aug. 1950), pp. 369-377. van Unnik in this valuable article characterizes the proclamation of the Lord's death in 1 Cor. 11.26 as Paul's paraphrase of 'Do this in remembrance of me'.

[2] Christians in Asia Minor in the second century regarded the Eucharist as a parallel to the Passover, and held a special celebration of it at the time of the Jewish Passover; see T. Zahn, *Introduction to the New Testament*, Eng. tr., iii, 1909, p. 274. The Ebionites observed the Eucharist as an annual feast, like the Jewish Passover, in memory of Christ's death, H. J. Schoeps, *Theologie und Geschichte des Judenchristentums*, 1949, p. 292; Epiphanius, *Haereses* 30.16, 1.

CHAPTER FIVE

TWO TYPES OF EUCHARIST?

In Luke and Acts there are several references to the breaking of bread. In Luke 24.35 and Acts 2.42 it is the noun which is used —'the breaking of bread' (ἡ κλάσις τοῦ ἄρτου); in Luke 24.30 and Acts 2.46; 20.7, 11 it is the verb.[1]

In Palestine it was customary not to cut the loaf with a knife, but to break it with the hands (Jer. 16.7; Lam. 4.4). Since every meal began with the 'breaking of bread', the expression was applied not only to the manual act in itself, but occasionally also to the opening rite of a meal, including the giving of thanks, the breaking and the distribution of the bread.[2] But it never denoted a *whole* meal until the New Testament. This new Christian usage demands an explanation. J. Jeremias[3] thinks the author of Acts is using veiled expressions, and that 'the breaking of bread' is a secret name for the Eucharist to hide the real nature of the rite from outsiders. It is not necessary, however, to suppose that this name has anything to do with the preservation of the *arcanum*; nor is it likely that the Christian use of the expressions is Luke's own invention, since their occurrence in his writings alone in the New Testament is probably accidental. There can be little doubt, however, that the Eucharist is meant. 'The breaking of bread' became a name for the Christian Lord's Supper because Jesus at his last Passover meal imposed a new and unexampled significance and importance on the bread. It was the earliest name for the Eucharist as the successor of the Jewish Passover. Thus Paul (1 Cor. 10.16) speaks of 'the bread which we break' at the Lord's Supper whose institution he describes in the next chapter.

---

[1] Acts 27.35 is irrelevant because it refers merely to breaking bread before taking nourishment.
[2] Babylonian Talmud, *Berakoth* 46a, 47a; G. Dalman, *Jesus-Jeshua*, Eng. tr., 1929, p. 136. [3] *Die Abendmahlsworte Jesu*, 2nd edn., 1949, pp. 64 f.

Two Types of Eucharist?

The meal at Troas over which Paul presided (Acts 20.7-11) was a eucharistic celebration. While we are told of the breaking of bread, no mention is made of wine. This does not imply that wine was not drunk. It would be surprising, to say the least, if Paul, who laid particular emphasis on the wine as denoting the covenant blood of Christ, had felt able to participate in a Eucharist from which the cup was absent.

The account of early Church life in Jerusalem in Acts 2.42-47 is not quite so clear, and some have thought that ordinary meals are meant. Yet there are strong reasons for the belief that here also the Eucharist is described. In verse 42 the mention of 'the breaking of bread' in the same breath as 'the prayers' suggests that the former is a meal of a religious nature, while in verse 46 'breaking bread in their homes' is placed on a level with the daily attendance of the Christians at the temple. As before, the silence about wine does not imply that it was not drunk. It cannot be denied, however, that this narrative certainly does not read like an account of a celebration in memory of the Lord's death such as is described by Paul in 1 Cor. 11, for 'they partook of food with *joy*'. This led F. Spitta[1] to differentiate between the joyful *agape* or love-feast such as we find in Acts 2.46, which was not held as if in obedience to an express command of the Lord and in which the thought of his death was not uppermost, and the Pauline kind of Eucharist in which these features were prominent.

But it is with the name of H. Lietzmann that the distinction between two types of Eucharist is especially associated. In his great work *Messe und Herrenmahl* (1926) he undertook to trace back to New Testament times the antecedents of the fourth-century Egyptian liturgy of Sarapion and of the third-century Roman liturgy of Hippolytus, from which, in his view, all later liturgies descend. The result is two distinct types of Eucharist. The Egyptian liturgy, dependent on the *Didache*, goes back ultimately to 'the breaking of bread' in Acts, which has no reference to the death of Christ and is unconnected with the Last Supper.

[1] *Zur Geschichte und Litteratur des Urchristentums*, i, 1893, pp. 289 f.

The Lord's Supper in the New Testament

This so-called Jerusalem type is the continuation of the ordinary meals of fellowship which the disciples had shared with the historical Jesus. It is marked by the joyful sense of the Lord's spiritual presence and by the confident expectation of his return at the Parousia. The Hippolytan liturgy is descended from the Pauline type of Eucharist, of which Lietzmann regarded Paul as the real creator. The apostle transformed the already existing Hellenistic sacramental Eucharist in accordance with a special revelation which made known to him the essential meaning of the Lord's Supper as a memorial of Christ's death. This type thus differs radically from the Jerusalem type both in its intrinsic nature and in its derivation from the Last Supper.[1]

The breaking of bread in Acts is also, according to Lietzmann, distinct from the Pauline kind of Lord's Supper in being a *communio sub una*. No wine is mentioned because none was drunk. Later examples of this are given[2]; and the shorter Lukan text (22.15-19*a*) is brought into the picture because it lacks the eucharistic cup. Here the evangelist desires to depict a Last Supper which cherishes eschatological hopes and in which the bread is the chief thing, as in the passages in Acts.[3] But the absence of the eucharistic cup from this Lukan account, which probably represents an independent tradition,[4] no more implies a wineless Eucharist than its absence from the narratives of the breaking of bread in Acts. Again, the absence from the longer text of Luke of the command,

---

[1] H. Lietzmann, op. cit., pp. 250-255. K. L. Schmidt reached similar conclusions in 'Abendmahl im Neuen Testament' in *Die Religion in Geschichte und Gegenwart*, 2nd edn., i, 1927, cols. 11-13. The writings of E. Lohmeyer on this subject ('Vom urchristlichen Abendmahl' in *Theologische Rundschau*, ix, 1937, pp. 168-227, 273-312; x, 1938, pp. 81-99; 'Das Abendmahl in der Urgemeinde' in *Journal of Biblical Literature*, lvi, 1937, pp. 217-252) are based on a similar principle of differentiation of two types: the bread-breaking of Galilaean tradition corresponds to Lietzmann's Jerusalem type, while Lohmeyer's Jerusalem type is that which, descended from the Last Supper, developed into the Pauline form of memorial feast.

[2] Lietzmann, op. cit., pp. 239 ff; e.g. *Acts of Peter* 5; *Acts of John* 85 f; 109 f. Water was sometimes substituted for wine, as by the Marcionites, Tatian's Encratites, and other sects. Such examples of the use of water instead of wine are, in the view of F. Spitta, op. cit., p. 290, remains of early Christian practice, and are not necessarily due to ascetic influence or special tendencies, but appeared as of heretical origin to the later Church with its now firmly established eucharistic usage; cf. also H. J. Schoeps, *Theologie und Geschichte des Judenchristentums*, 1949, pp. 194 f.

[3] Lietzmann, op. cit., pp. 215-217.   [4] See above, pp. 42 f.

Two Types of Eucharist?

'Do this in remembrance of me' after the saying over the cup might be held to have some connection with the supposed wineless Eucharists in Acts. This fact, combined with Paul's limitation 'as often as you drink it' (1 Cor. 11.25), has been regarded as an indication that wine was only seldom used.[1] But we have seen that the command to repeat after the wine is a creation of Paul himself, and formed no part of the tradition used by him, and followed independently by Luke,[2] who is, therefore, not omitting anything. And the words 'as often as you drink it', so far from implying the rare use of wine at the Lord's Supper, mean 'every time you drink it' in the sense that wine is as obligatory as the bread. This is clear from the next verse, in which the same words as often as' recur: every celebration, which consists both of bread and of wine, is a proclamation of the Lord's death. No doubt Paul wished to emphasize the importance of the wine in accordance with his view of the Last Supper as the inauguration of a new covenant ratified in the blood of Christ. But there is no reason to suppose that the cup did not form part of the primitive breadbreaking because it is not mentioned.

Paul was not the originator of the type of Eucharist which was predominantly a feast in memory of Christ's death, because the first 'Do this in remembrance of me' belonged to a tradition he had received.[3] Moreover, this pre-Pauline feature of remembrance will not be due to the influence of Hellenistic memorial feasts in honour of the dead, but to the fact that the eucharistic gatherings of the primitive *Palestinian* Church were descended from the Last Supper which, as a Passover, was especially characterized by the central element of remembrance. It seems, then, that the antithesis 'primitive-Palestinian breaking of bread in Acts' and 'Hellenistic-Pauline Eucharist' is false, and that the element of remembrance of Christ's death was just as probably present in the former as in the latter. Certainly the breaking of bread was 'with 'joy', the word used ($\dot{\alpha}\gamma\alpha\lambda\lambda\iota\alpha\sigma\iota\varsigma$) denoting especially eschatological

---

[1] A. Schlatter, according to J. Jeremias, op. cit., p. 28, n. 9.
[2] See above, p. 44.   [3] See above, pp. 26, 36.

joy.¹ While this joyful expectation of the greater Messianic meal to be shared with the glorified Lord in the Kingdom of God had relegated the memory of his death somewhat to the background, the same eschatological outlook persists in the type of Lord's Supper of which we know more (Mark 14.25), and Paul himself reveals his knowledge of it. 'For as often as you eat this bread and drink the cup, you proclaim the Lord's death until he comes' (1 Cor. 11.26). This waiting for the coming of Christ found expression in the primitive Aramaic prayer *Marana tha*, 'Our Lord, come'. If it occurs in a definitely eucharistic context in the *Didache* 10.6, a document classed by Lietzmann as a representative of the non-Pauline kind of Eucharist, Paul also knows it (1 Cor. 16.22), and we are to recognize a direct reminiscence of it in 1 Cor. 11.26—'For as often as you eat this bread and drink the cup, you proclaim the Lord's death *until he comes*'.

The validity of the rigid distinction between two alleged types of Eucharist is, then, greatly weakened as regards both origin and content; while if the so-called Jerusalem type is also connected with the Last Supper, wine will have been drunk even though it is unmentioned because it is included in the 'breaking of bread' which is the name for the whole meal.

Nevertheless Paul did, of course, make changes. At Corinth he introduced reforms into the eucharistic celebrations which he discovered had degenerated into exhibitions of selfishness and drunkenness. The custom at Corinth, as elsewhere, was for the special eucharistic partaking of bread and wine to take place during the course of a meal of fellowship, the *agape* (to use the later term), called by Paul 'the Lord's Supper' ($\kappa\nu\rho\iota\alpha\kappa\grave{o}\nu$ $\delta\epsilon\hat{\iota}\pi\nu o\nu$, 1 Cor. 11.20).² That is why other food, such as fish, is sometimes mentioned in connection with the Eucharist. To check the abuses Paul ordered the Corinthians to take necessary nourishment in their own homes before coming to the gathering (1 Cor. 11.22, 34). Thereby the first step was taken in the transformation of a real

---

[1] R. Bultmann in G. Kittel's *Theologisches Wörterbuch zum Neuen Testament*, i, 1933, pp. 19 f.   [2] In Jude 12 we hear of still worse abuses at the love-feasts or *agapae*.

Two Types of Eucharist?

meal which included the eucharistic remembrance of the Lord's death and the prayer for his return into a purely cultic celebration.

A fruitful line of approach, which seems to me to be correct in essentials, is that of O. Cullmann, who, in *La signification de la Sainte-Cène dans le christianisme primitif*,[1] developed a theory of eucharistic origins which differs in two important respects from that of Lietzmann. Firstly, Cullmann does not find the direct origin of the Jerusalem 'breaking of bread' in the daily common meals of Jesus with his disciples, but in the resurrection appearances of the Lord at the meals of the disciples between Easter and his ascension.[2] Secondly, while Lietzmann denied that there was any connection of the Jerusalem type with the Last Supper, Cullmann rightly regards this as the common origin of both types of Eucharist, if indirectly in the case of the Jerusalem type.

The passages to be examined are Luke 24.30-35, 36-43; John 21.9 ff; Acts 1.4; 10.41; and Rev. 3.20.

The joy characteristic of the breaking of bread in the earliest community (Acts 2.46) was inspired by the memory of the appearance of the risen Lord at the disciples' meals together, beginning with that recorded in Luke 24.36-43. Here the only food mentioned is fish; in the narrative of the appearance of the Lord to the disciples by the sea of Tiberias in John 21 fish and bread are eaten. The fish, as in later Christian art, is a definitely eucharistic symbol. The bread and fish of John 21 turn up again in the narrative of the feeding of the multitude, which the fourth evangelist obviously regarded as eucharistic, because he appended the eucharistic discourse on the bread of life.[3] The eucharistic signifi-

---

[1] Reprinted from *Revue d'Histoire et de Philosophie religieuses*, 1936, pp. 1-22; cf. also *Urchristentum und Gottesdienst*, 2nd edn., 1950, pp. 17 ff.

[2] The notion that the early Eucharist was connected with appearances of the risen Christ is, of course, not new; cf., e.g. F. Spitta, op. cit., pp. 292 f; M. Goguel, *L'église primitive*, 1948, p. 361.

[3] Further evidence that chapter 21 is eucharistic is the close similarity between verses 15-17 ('lovest thou me?') and the emphasis on love (ἀγάπη) in the undoubted eucharistic framework of chapters 13-17, where also, in 14.21, there is discernible an echo of the association between the Eucharist and the appearance of the risen Christ. 'He who has my commandments and keeps them, he it is who loves me; and he who loves me will be loved by my Father, and I will love him and *manifest myself to him*' (cf. 14.23).

cance of food other than bread and wine is connected with the fact that the first Eucharists formed part of an ordinary meal. These two narratives of resurrection appearances testify to this; while in the story in Luke 24.30-35 of how the Lord was known to Cleopas and his companion in 'the breaking of bread' (the oldest name for the Eucharist) we have, though in a different form, another similar ante-dating of the Eucharist embedded in a reminiscence of the early Church's experience of the presence of the risen Lord at the common eucharistic meal.

The first few verses of Acts relate the coming of the risen Christ to his disciples during the forty days until the ascension. In verse 4 the word συναλιζόμενος, which, if given its classical meaning, would be translated 'being assembled together with them' as in the Authorised and Revised Versions, can also mean 'taking salt with them', and therefore means a eucharistic meal, just as the later Jewish Christians who celebrated with bread and salt called their Eucharist 'a sharing of salt'.[1] That this is the correct interpretation is borne out by the statement in Peter's address to Cornelius, that Jesus was raised up by God on the third day and made manifest 'not to all the people, but to us who were chosen by God as witnesses who *ate and drank with him after he rose from the dead*' (Acts 10.41). This looks back to Acts 1.4.[2]

Such was the experience of the first believers, whose joy was aroused by the vivid consciousness of the presence of the risen Lord at their meals, and crowned by the expectation of the fulfilment in the Messianic meal in the Kingdom of God. It is very probable that Rev. 3.20, 'Behold, I stand at the door and knock; if anyone hears my voice and opens the door, I will come in to him and sup with him, and he with me', witnesses to the belief that as in the first post-resurrection days so now Christ condescends to be present with his own when they assemble to break bread.

[1] O. Cullmann, *La signification de la Sainte-Cène dans le christianisme primitif*, 1936, pp. 8 f; *Urchristentum und Gottesdienst*, 2nd edn., 1950, p. 19; see also H. J. Schoeps, op. cit., pp. 195, 292, 468, 473.
[2] With Acts 10.42 f compare also Acts 1.4 f and Luke 24.44-49.

Two Types of Eucharist?

Cullmann holds that this joyful breaking of bread is connected, though indirectly, with the Last Supper. It was inspired by the appearances of the risen Christ at the community meals, beginning with that recorded in Luke 24.36-43, which was the sequel to the Last Supper. Here the disciples were presumably assembled in the same upper room, with their last meal in the company of Jesus fresh in their memories. The impact of the resurrection experience was such that at first their thought of the death of Jesus was pushed into the background, and their psychological state was overwhelming joy at his spiritual presence. This joy, indeed, with its eschatological outlook on even greater glories to come, continued as a predominant feature in the Church's Eucharists. But to suppose that there was no thought or remembrance of the Master's death is an unwarranted assumption; and psychologically it is improbable. We have already given reasons for the view that the idea of remembrance of Christ's death was no invention of Paul's, but existed before him; and that, although to be sure it is not actually mentioned any more than the partaking of wine, it must long have been present in the *Palestinian* as well as in the Hellenistic communities. It is very probable, especially in view of the dependence of both so-called types of Eucharist on the Last Supper, that what Paul did was to lay a renewed emphasis on the remembrance of the death of Christ which was already present, but which at Corinth was in danger of being forgotten—not to mention brotherly generosity and good manners. In seeking to correct these abuses by counselling the hungry to eat at home first, Paul took the initial step in the separation of the specifically eucharistic celebration from the meal of which it formed part; and this celebration, consisting of 'this bread' and 'the cup of the Lord' (1 Cor. 11.27), was to 'proclaim the Lord's death until he comes'.

CHAPTER SIX

PAUL'S TEACHING ON THE LORD'S SUPPER

THE teaching of Paul on the Lord's Supper is not confined to his account of its institution in 1 Cor. 11.23-26, the significance of which has been discussed in earlier chapters. Of the greatest importance is his rebuke of abuses at the Lord's Supper in the church of Corinth (verses 17-22) which impelled him to remind the members of the tradition as he had delivered it to them, and the following warnings of the results of the continuation of this conduct (verses 27-34). Of equal importance is 1 Cor. 10.1-22, while 1 Cor. 5.6-8 contains an important allusion to the Eucharist. We shall treat these passages in the order in which they appear in the Epistle.

1 Cor. 5.6-8

The occasion for what the apostle here writes is a flagrant case of immorality in the Corinthian church. The excuse that this is, after all, only an isolated instance is invalid, and the offender must be expelled (verses 2, 13), otherwise the whole church, as the lump of dough, will be contaminated by the presence of this small amount of leaven.[1] Therefore, just as the Jews before Passover clear out all traces of leaven from their dwellings, the believers at Corinth must remove from their midst the leaven of evil, so as to correspond to their true nature of unleavened bread, cleansed of all the impurities of their past pagan life out of which they have been delivered like the Jews of old from Egypt. For they, too, have a paschal victim, Christ, who was sacrificed once and for all. 'So let us keep the feast, not with the old leaven, the leaven

---

[1] With 5.6 cf. Gal. 5.9, where the occurrence of the same saying in an identical form suggests that Paul is repeating a proverb.

of malice and wickedness, but with the unleavened bread of sincerity and truth.' This sentence does not refer to the Eucharist as a Christian counterpart to the Jewish Passover, but describes the whole Christian life as a festival which must be celebrated with purity of conduct. It has been suggested that the use of Passover language in this passage is due to the approach of the Passover season. But there is more to be said.

It is probable that the idea of Christ as a paschal lamb was quite familiar to the Christians of Corinth,[1] because it was common property in the early Church, as we know from the New Testament.[2] Since it probably goes back to the Lord's comparison of himself with the paschal lamb at the Last Supper, the phrase 'Christ our Passover has been sacrificed' is an allusion to the Eucharist. In this, however, Paul may well represent the same chronology as that of the Fourth Gospel, according to which Christ was a paschal victim because he was crucified on the afternoon of Nisan 14th, at the very time when the lambs were sacrificed in the temple. Some support for this possibility is provided by 1 Cor. 15.20, where the risen Lord is called the 'first fruits' of the dead. This means that the day of the resurrection, our Sunday, corresponded to Nisan 16th, on which the first sheaf of barley was offered in the temple. This would put the crucifixion on Nisan 14th, as in the Fourth Gospel.

1 *Cor.* 10.1-22.

In a manner which seems rather strange to us Paul here reminds the Corinthians that the Israelites received the counterpart of the Christian sacraments of baptism and the Eucharist, but that did not save them from the dire consequences of evil, particularly idolatry. Their experiences were a warning that the sacraments are not an automatic protection from punishment for disloyalty, as exemplified in idolatry, to which the apostle comes in verses 14-21.

---

[1] J. Weiss, *Der erste Korintherbrief*, 10th edn., 1925, pp. 135 f.
[2] The Fourth Gospel; 1 Peter 1.19; Rev. 5.6.

The Lord's Supper in the New Testament

Paul draws on Jewish traditions in finding analogies to the two Christian sacraments in the experiences of the wilderness generation. The pillar of cloud *preceded* the Israelites by day (Ex. 13.21 f); but there is a tradition more apposite to the idea of baptism in Ps. 105.39, where the cloud is a *covering*, and in Wisdom 19.7, which says the cloud 'shadowed the camp'.[1] Similarly, the biblical narrative of the crossing of the Red Sea, in which the waters parted for the Israelites who went over on dry ground (Ex. 14.21 f), does not supply a sufficiently close analogy to baptism. This is provided in the midrashic explanations that the waters parted so as to form a sort of tunnel for the Israelites to pass through.[2] Thus Paul can find in the experiences of the wilderness generation an analogy to Christian baptism: 'all were baptized into Moses in the cloud and in the sea'.

In verse 3 Paul goes on to the even more important analogy to the Eucharist, which is his primary concern in the whole of this passage. 'And all ate the same supernatural food[3] and all drank the same supernatural drink;[3] for they drank from the supernatural rock[3] which followed them, and the rock was Christ.' The supernatural food is the manna (Ex. 16.4, 14-18), which is supernatural because it came from heaven, but also because it is the type of the eucharistic bread. Emphasis is laid on all having partaken of the same supernatural food and drink because both the few who were saved and those who 'were overthrown in the wilderness' had taken it, and also because at the Eucharist the whole body of believers receives the same bread and wine.

For the Israelite counterpart to the eucharistic wine Paul, as in the case of baptism, has recourse to traditions which had grown up round the biblical narratives. Ex. 17.6 describes how water gushed forth from the rock in Horeb to supply the people with drink when Moses struck it. The legend of the following rock, which Paul identifies with Christ, is a Rabbinic tradition based on

---
[1] See Strack-Billerbeck, *Kommentar zum Neuen Testament aus Talmud und Midrasch* iii, 1926, p. 405.
[2] Strack-Billerbeck, op. cit., iii, pp. 405 f.
[3] So Moffatt, Goodspeed, and the American Revised Standard Version.

Paul's Teaching on the Lord's Supper

identification of the well to which the Israelites came after a long wandering (Num. 21.16) with the spring which rushed forth from the rock when struck by Moses (Num. 20.7 ff). The Targum Onkelos (Num. 21.19) speaks of the spring going with the Israelites down the valleys and up the hills.[1] But the nearest parallel may be in a passage in the Tosephta,[2] which J. Héring[3] thinks states that the rock itself followed the Israelites.[4] However this may be, Paul knew a tradition to this effect, and interprets the rock as the Messiah. The drink is supernatural because it is supplied by the supernatural rock, Christ, and is the type of the eucharistic wine. The reason for Paul's identification of the rock with Christ is to be found in his Wisdom Christology (1 Cor. 1.24, 30; Col. 1.15-17). Philo says the rock was the Wisdom of God.[5] Thus Paul, who identified Christ with Widsom, can say that the rock which followed the Israelites was Christ.

Yet despite the supernatural food most of the Israelites were overthrown in the wilderness, because their idolatry, immorality and disloyalty provoked the anger of God. The same thing will happen to you (verse 22), warns the apostle, if you are guilty of similar sins; you will not escape because you have been duly baptized and have partaken of the Eucharist. There is no magical power in the sacraments. Such seems to be Paul's view, as we shall further see when we come to 1 Cor. 11.27-34, where it is not the elements but the Lord who punishes those who abuse his Supper.

'Therefore, my beloved, flee from idolatry' (verse 14). Some of the Corinthian converts saw no harm in a kind of religious syncretism, and did not consider it inconsistent with their Christian confession to continue attendance at heathen temples. Even if some of them had ceased to believe in the heathen gods, what

---

[1] So also Targum Pseudo-Jonathan and the Fragment Targum; see the translations of these passages in J. W. Etheridge, *The Targums of the Pentateuch*, ii, 1865, pp. 300, 413.   [2] *Sukkah* 3.11.
[3] *La première épître de saint Paul aux Corinthiens*, 1949, p. 79.
[4] Héring gives the reasons for this view in a note on p. 79. The passage, however, seems to end by saying that the *spring* was where the Israelites were.
[5] *Legum Allegoriae* ii. 86, and *Quod deterius potiori insidiari soleat* 115

harm could there be in keeping up the old associations? But Paul is quite definite about it. The question is not a matter of indifference, in which everyone may please himself. 'You cannot drink the cup of the Lord and the cup of demons; you cannot partake of the table of the Lord and the table of demons' (verse 21). He points to the fact that in Judaism the priests by eating some of the sacrifices are brought into close association with (the God of) the altar (verse 18). But more pertinent to the argument is the pagan practice. A man who had sacrificed an animal to a pagan deity was able to use part of the food for a meal for his friends within the temple precincts.[1] These meals were sacramental in nature, because the guests believed that by eating some of the same food which had been offered to the god upon his altar they were brought into a specially close relation with him, and might thus expect to receive benefits from him. What harm could there be in attending these banquets? Does Paul, his opponents ask, think that idol-food is anything or that an idol is anything? (verse 19). The apostle's answer is curiously inconsistent. 'No, but what the heathen sacrifice they sacrifice to demons and not to God; I do not want you to be partners with demons.' The contradiction is typically Jewish: the idols and the deities they represent are nothing, yet these gods are actually demons.[2] Paul is in no doubt as to the existence and malign influence of these powers[3]; to participate in their worship and cultic meals is to lay oneself open to their control, whatever one's beliefs about them may be. Moreover, the demons belong to the hostile spiritual forces of Satan, upon which Christ is waging war. How, then, is it possible to have fellowship both with Christ and with the demons? To eat at the table of pagan gods is to make a mockery of the Eucharist. The Lord, too, has a table and a cup, and by eating at his table we are brought into close communion with him. 'The cup of blessing which we bless, is it not a means of sharing (κοινωνία) in the blood

[1] Examples are given by H. Lietzmann, *An Die Korinther I-II*, 4th edn., 1949, pp. 49 f.
[2] Cf. Strack-Billerbeck, op. cit., iii, pp. 51 f.
[3] Cf. Rom. 8.38; 1 Cor. 2.8; Gal. 4.9; Eph. 6.11 f; Col. 2.8.

Paul's Teaching on the Lord's Supper

of Christ? The bread which we break, is it not a means of sharing in the body of Christ?' (verse 16).[1]

The cup of blessing is a means of sharing in the blood of Christ because believers in drinking of the cup over which Christ gave thanks appropriate to themselves the benefits of his sacrificial death (Rom. 3.25; 5.9); they have communion with Christ crucified and risen again, because they show themselves ready to share in his sufferings (cf. Rom. 8.17). There must also be present to Paul's mind his idea of the cup as the new covenant in the blood of Christ (1 Cor. 11.25). To partake of this cup is a criterion of readiness to share in his blood, in his suffering.

In what sense is the bread a means of sharing in the body of Christ? 'The body of Christ' here is certainly the Church (1 Cor. 12.27).[2] The breaking and eating of the common loaf is a means of fellowship with one's brethren in Christ, and confirms believers as members of the one body of Christ, the Church into which they were baptized (1 Cor. 12.13). This oneness is demonstrated and reaffirmed by sharing in the common loaf.

Basic to Paul's teaching is his doctrine, the result of his own vivid personal experience, of union with Christ by faith. Christ dwells in the believer (Rom. 8.10; Gal. 2.20; Col. 1.27), and he is 'in Christ' (2 Cor. 5.17). But for the individual to be in Christ (or for Christ to be living in him) is not a purely personal faith-relationship; he is in the body of Christ which consists of others who have come to enjoy a like relationship. He and they have been baptized into Christ (Gal. 3.27), who is one body (1 Cor. 12.12 f). Since to Paul, then, Christ is not only the individual Jesus Christ, but a corporate personality whose visible, material manifestation is the Church which is his body, union with Christ finds its expression in this societary way in membership of the body of Christ.

It is hard to resist the conclusion that Paul's teaching about the

---

[1] The rhythm suggests that this may be a liturgical formula; cf. M. Goguel, *L'église primitive*, 1948, p. 355.
[2] F. J. Leenhardt, *Le sacrement de la Sainte Cène*, 1948, p. 78 n. strangely sees no reference to the Church in this verse.

Church as the body of Christ was suggested to him by that form of the tradition of the Last Supper which records that Jesus said of the bread, 'This is my body'. He gives the reason why the breaking of bread is a means of sharing in the body of Christ. 'Because there is one loaf, we who are many are one body; for we all partake of the one loaf' (verse 17). Sharing the one loaf makes us one body—Christ's body. The words, 'The bread which we break, is it not a means of sharing in the body of Christ?' must mean not alone fellowship with fellow members in the Church and with the risen Christ who is spiritually present within it, but a sharing in what happened to the human body of Jesus; they form a parallel to sharing in his blood, and refer even more emphatically than the latter to the death of Christ and to a sharing in it, because the Church *is* his body. This double meaning of 'the body of Christ' recurs in 1 Cor. 11.27-29.[1] The two expressions in 1 Cor. 10.16 together denote the corporate aspect of the individual's experience of 'the fellowship of his sufferings' (Phil. 3.10). Though communion with Christ in the Eucharist may be secondary chronologically to union with Christ by faith, it is questionable whether Paul recognized any inherent precedence of the latter over the former, or made any clear-cut distinction between them, for he held the Eucharist to be essential to the Church as a command from the Lord himself.

In Paul we see the beginnings of a new emphasis on the eucharistic elements themselves. But they are a means of sharing in the body and blood of Christ, and are not equated with them. They possess no inherent mysterious power; and Paul does not speak, like the fourth evangelist, of eating the flesh and drinking the blood of Christ.

1 *Cor.* 11.18-34

The apostle begins by criticizing the assemblies in which the

---

[1] If verse 16 in our chapter is taken to be a *pre-Pauline* liturgical formula, 'the body of Christ' would originally have the same meaning as in the Lord's own declaration, 'This is my body', and Paul adds his own doctrine of the Church as the body of Christ.

Paul's Teaching on the Lord's Supper

parties or cliques, probably the same as those he has dealt with earlier in this letter, disrupt the spirit of unity in Christ. He even calls them 'factions', a term which draws attention to the leaders of the cliques, who were perhaps guilty of some deliberate interference with the eucharistic teaching which he had previously (verse 23) imparted to the Corinthian church. At all events, it was not the Lord's Supper that they ate when they assembled as a church, because brotherly fellowship was absent. The Lord's Supper here is the whole of the common meal, concluding with the Eucharist proper. Social inequality was clearly one of the root causes of the disorderliness of the Lord's Supper at Corinth. The rich began to eat without waiting for the arrival of the poorer brethren, who would be late because of their occupations.[1] And they ate and drank to excess, while others went hungry. In doing so they humiliated their less fortunate brethren, and despised the church of God (verse 22). The place to feast was at home. This behaviour was totally at variance with the meaning of the Lord's Supper as he had taught it to them. Paul reminds the Corinthians of the tradition he had passed on to them in verses 23-26, a passage which has already been discussed in detail in earlier chapters. They needed to be reminded sharply of the solemn nature of the eucharistic breaking of bread which was in great danger of being swallowed up by the festive gathering which led up to it. They must remember above all that it commemorates the *death* of the Lord. For this reason Paul orders that the common meal is to cease being a satisfaction of hunger, lest the result of their assembling should be condemnation (verse 34). He thus initiated a process which ended in the separation of the eucharistic celebration from the community meal.

We go back to Paul's admonitions and warnings (verses 27-30), which are very severe.

'So whoever eats the bread or drinks the cup of the Lord unworthily will be blameworthy as regards the body and blood of the Lord. Let a man examine himself, and so eat of the bread

---

[1] J. Héring, op. cit., p. 99.

and drink of the cup. For he who eats and drinks without discerning the body eats and drinks judgment upon himself. For this reason many among you are weak and ill, and some have died.'

There are two main lines of interpretation of this difficult passage.

According to the former of these, eating the bread and drinking the cup unworthily means regarding the elements as ordinary food instead of as the body and blood of the Lord, and is a crime against the body and blood. Failure to discern the body is the same thing —inability to distinguish the body of Christ from an ordinary piece of bread. The diseases and deaths in the Corinthian church, which Paul attributes to unworthy conduct at the Lord's Supper are, on this view, produced by a sort of automatic reaction of the elements which, instead of being a 'medicine of immortality' (Ignatius, *Eph.* 20.2) become a deadly poison.[1] But it is very questionable whether Paul's conception is as realist as this. He does not speak of eating the body and drinking the blood of the Lord.[2]

The second way of understanding the passage has much more to commend it. To quote J. Moffatt: 'The charge against the irreverent Corinthians is not that they failed to distinguish any consecrated elements in the meal, or that they undervalued the sacrificial side of communion, but that they forgot what the Body meant as they acted so selfishly towards their humbler fellow-Christians. Paul reiterates at this point what he had urged in 20 and 21, but in terms now of the Body.'[3] Eating and drinking without discerning the body, which is the same as doing so in an unworthy manner, means conduct at the Lord's Supper which is due to failure to recognize the Church for what it is, the body of

---

[1] H. Lietzmann, op. cit., p. 59; cf. J. Weiss, op. cit., pp. 290 f.
[2] Among exponents of this first view of the passage may be mentioned, besides Lietzmann and J. Weiss, M. Goguel, *L'eucharistie des origines à Justin Martyr*, 1910, pp. 177 f, and J. Héring, op. cit., p. 104.
[3] *The First Epistle of Paul to the Corinthians*, 1938, p. 171. Cf. also C. A. A. Scott, *Christianity according to St Paul*, 1927, pp. 189, 197; W. G. Kümmel in H. Lietzmann, op. cit., p. 186; F. J. Leenhardt, op. cit., pp. 87 f, who, however, adopts the improbable explanation of verse 27b as denoting a share in the responsibility for Christ's death, comparing Heb. 6.6 and 10.29.

Paul's Teaching on the Lord's Supper

Christ, in which the living Lord is present. The conduct in question is that with which Paul has already charged the Corinthians, conduct which impelled him to remind them of the true nature and significance of the Supper. He means especially that selfish lack of consideration for others and that eating and drinking to excess which involve contempt of the Church of God (verse 22). 'The body', then, in verse 29 is the Church. But because such behaviour dishonours the Church as the body of Christ, it is a crime against the Lord of the Church himself, a sin against his body and blood (verse 27) given in sacrifice in order that believers may belong to the risen Lord who is present in the Church his body (cf. Rom. 7.4). The sicknesses and deaths attributed by the apostle to abuse of the Lord's Supper are not caused by the reaction of eucharistic elements endowed with some mysterious potency, but are a punishment inflicted by the Lord. That this is so is clear from verse 32, in which Paul closes on a gentler note. Although these afflictions are the judgments of the Lord, they are not final condemnation, but chastisements to bring offenders to a better frame of mind, so as to escape being involved in the condemnation of the world.

CHAPTER SEVEN

JOHANNINE EUCHARISTIC DOCTRINE

AMONG the many notable differences between the Fourth Gospel and the Synoptics is the absence from the former of an account of the institution of the Lord's Supper. Various attempts have been made to account for this radical departure from precedent.

Some have suggested that the fourth evangelist is anti-sacramentalist, or at least is not interested in sacraments as of primary importance in the life of the Church. A recent advocate of this view is R. Bultmann, who in his commentary represents the evangelist as at best negative in his attitude to the sacraments.[1] This position seems to me quite untenable. The Fourth Gospel is, on the contrary, the most sacramentalist of all the New Testament writings, and this chapter will show that it assigns a vital role to the Eucharist.

A second view is that John is silent on the institution of the Eucharist because he wishes to conceal knowledge of the rite and its sacred formulae from the uninitiated.[2] But this motive of concealment belongs to a later period.[3]

A third view, advanced by E. Lohmeyer,[4] is that John associates the institution of the Eucharist not with the Last Supper, but with the feeding of the multitude, and so belongs to the Galilaean tradition.[5] For this reason the eucharistic teaching is transferred to the narrative of the feeding from its natural place in the account of the events in the upper room on our Lord's last night. While it is true that the evangelist attaches his most important and most

---
[1] *Das Evangelium des Johannes*, 1950 (=1941), p. 360.
[2] See W. L. Knox, *Some Hellenistic Elements in Primitive Christianity*, 1944, p. 66; J. Jeremias, *Die Abendmahlsworte Jesu*, 2nd edn., 1949, pp. 59, 67.
[3] See above, p. 39, n.3, and cf. R. Bultmann, op. cit., p. 360, n.4.
[4] 'Das Abendmahl in der Urgemeinde' in *Journal of Biblical Literature*, lvi, 1937, p. 249.
[5] See above, p. 58, n.1.

Johannine Eucharistic Doctrine

distinctive eucharistic teaching to the traditional story of the feeding of the multitude, the reason for this is to be found elsewhere than in any theory of two types of Eucharist in the New Testament Church.

Characteristic of the fourth evangelist is his allusive way of referring to what is explicit in the tradition known to him, and to us through the Synoptic Gospels. The baptism of Jesus is not recorded, but hinted at in the testimony of John the Baptist that he had seen the Spirit descend upon him (1.32 f). In Mark 14.34 f Jesus in Gethsemane tells his friends that his soul is very sorrowful, and prays that 'the hour' might pass from him. In John in quite a different context Jesus confesses that his soul is troubled, and asks whether he should pray, 'Father, save me from this hour' (12.27). The opinion of some bystanders that the voice which others thought was thunder was the voice of an angel is an echo of the tradition represented in Luke 22.43 that an angel strengthened the Lord in his agony in the garden. The ascension is alluded to as a well known and accepted object of belief (John 3.13; 6.62; 20.17), while in 1.51 there is a reflection of the belief in the return of the Son of Man 'with the holy angels' (Mark 8.38). Because this evangelist is interested primarily not in history for its own sake, but in its theological interpretation, he feels himself to be free from the constraint of chronology in incorporating into his work items from familiar traditions. That is why he is able to transfer his reminiscences of the scene in Gethsemane to a different context, and to picture Jesus in his discussion with Nicodemus referring to his ascension as though it had already taken place. The writer, who does not record directly the baptism of Jesus, gives his teaching on baptism indirectly in several different places (3.1 ff; 4.1 ff; 13.1-20; 19.34); in exactly the same way his silence on the institution of the Lord's Supper is more than compensated for by the eucharistic teaching introduced in other parts of the Gospel.

The most important source for Johannine eucharistic doctrine is the discourse on the bread of life in the sixth chapter. Connected with the question why the Fourth Gospel omits the institution of the Eucharist at the Last Supper—an omission which is partially, but only partially explained by its allusive nature—is the problem of accounting for the association of its really vital teaching on the subject with the miracle of the feeding.

The starting point is the apologetic purpose of the author. The Eucharist was the object of intense controversy. The sacrament, which has always been misunderstood by Jews, had to be defended against attacks from the side of Judaism. 'The Jews' in this Gospel are in this respect, as in others, the arch-enemies. The whole discourse in chapter six is an argument with Jewish objectors, and the stage is aptly set in the synagogue at Capernaum. But there were also those within the Church itself who were hostile to the Eucharist. We learn a little later from Ignatius[1] of people who abstained from the sacrament because they refused to accept the Church's belief in the presence of the flesh and blood of Christ in the elements. After the conclusion of the discourse in the synagogue, we read of the difficulties felt by many of the disciples themselves, and of their desertion of Jesus (6.60-66). The evangelist, indirectly, as is his custom, is saying exactly the same thing as Ignatius; people were leaving the Church, and no doubt they are the kind of people of whose apostasy we learn in the Johannine Epistles (1 John 4.1-3; 2 John 7): desiring a more 'spiritual' religion, they refused to acknowledge that the Son of God had come *in the flesh*.[2] The scene in the upper room, hallowed by sacred associations, would have been totally unsuitable for the presentation of a defence of the Eucharist. Besides, while a treacherous disciple was certainly present, there were no unbelieving Jews to refute; but what more likely place in which to find them than the crowd which melts into the 'Jews' in the synagogue?

The eucharistic teaching in the sixth chapter is connected with the anti-docetic purpose of the Gospel. The signs which are recorded out of many more which Jesus did have been chosen to

---

[1] *Smyrn.* 5 f.
[2] Cf. E. C. Hoskyns, *The Fourth Gospel*, 2nd edn., 1950 (=1947), pp. 301 f.

Johannine Eucharistic Doctrine

induce belief, whose reward is eternal life, that Jesus is the Messiah, the Son of God (20.31); and the Son of God in the body of the Gospel is the Word which became *flesh* in the prologue (1.14). Moreover, the teaching of this Gospel is that the Christ who became flesh and lived upon earth is identical with the Christ who is present in the Eucharist.[1] Hence the emphasis on the eucharistic flesh and blood. The apostolic eye-witnesses had the inestimable privilege of beholding the glory of the incarnate Word in the life of Jesus of Nazareth (1.14). But the evangelist wishes to impress upon his readers that the presence of Christ in the Eucharist is just as real as his physical presence was to the apostles. In fact, it is more real, because believers are able to eat the flesh and drink the blood of Christ, to enjoy a communion with him, now that he has ascended to the Father, which was impossible during his earthly life.

We are thus brought to another reason for the absence of the institution of the sacrament at the Last Supper. Just as the Jews at their Passover ate the flesh of a victim which had been slain, so the Eucharist could not take place until after the death of Christ, the paschal lamb. He is the Lamb of God at the beginning of the Gospel (1.29, 36); at the end he is the paschal lamb whose bones are not broken, that the scripture might be fulfilled (19.36; Ex. 12.46; Num. 9.12). In John, therefore, the Last Supper is not a Passover meal. It is antedated by twenty-four hours, so that the connection with the Passover is not, as in the Synoptics, that the Last Supper was a Passover, but that Christ is the perfect paschal victim, crucified simultaneously with the sacrifice of the lambs in the temple. The conception that the Spirit was not given until after the glorification of Jesus (7.39) is also operative here. The Last Supper is not regarded as the occasion of the institution of the Eucharist, which was only possible after the death of Christ because he must first die to re-enter the heavenly world so as to impart the powers of the Spirit which bestow eternal life.[2]

[1] Cf. O. Cullmann, *Urchristentum und Gottesdienst*, 2nd edn., 1950, pp. 57 f.
[2] M. Goguel, *L'eucharistie des origines à Justin Martyr*, 1910, p. 212; *L'église primitive*, 1948, p. 374.

Finally, we must take into account the fundamental attitude of the Fourth Gospel to the redemptive work of Christ. Paul lays the emphasis on the redemptive power of the *death* of Christ, with whom the believer is united by faith. This faith-union is actualized in the sacraments: in baptism as burial with Christ in death and as resurrection with him to a new life, and in the Eucharist as a means of sharing in the dying body and blood of Christ. But in the Fourth Gospel the whole incarnation and life of Christ are redemptive, and his death is his deliberately chosen path to glory. Faith-union is with the living and glorified Christ; parallel to this is sacramental communion with him in partaking of his flesh and blood. The Eucharist is brought into association with the incarnation and not primarily with the Passion. In the sixth chapter the living Jesus of history, the Word made flesh, who feeds a multitude with bread and fish, is identical with the Christ of the Eucharist who offers his flesh as the real food.

We turn to the various eucharistic passages.

The Wedding at Cana, 2.1-11

Jesus at first refuses the request of his mother to supply wine, because his 'hour' had not yet come. Here 'hour', as elsewhere in the Gospel, is the hour of his Passion or glorification (12.23), when he returns to the Father. So on two occasions he was not arrested 'because his hour had not yet come' (7.30; 8.20), and he declined to follow his brothers' advice to go to Jerusalem because his 'time' had not yet come (7.6, 8). The hour which at Cana had not yet arrived has come in 13.1, and therefore it is time to institute the Eucharist, which the evangelist, because of his view that the Eucharist must be subsequent to the death of Christ, does not record directly, but in the allegory of the foot-washing. Yet despite his refusal to supply the deficiency of wine, Jesus proceeds to change water into wine. There is no real contradiction. He performs the material miracle his mother desired, but it is only a pointer to the greater miracle for which the time has not yet come. The changing of water into wine is a sign (verse 11), the first of

Johannine Eucharistic Doctrine

many. It is a sign because it points forward to the Eucharist.[1] The wine represents the eucharistic wine, the blood of Christ which cleanses from sin, and replaces the purificatory water and washings of Judaism (verse 6).

The Cana narrative is thus closely parallel to the miracle of feeding in the sixth chapter: here the miraculous supply of wine, the blood of Christ, there the miraculous supply of bread, the flesh of Christ. The aspect of the Eucharist which is here implicitly stressed, that of purification, reappears in two other eucharistic passages. In 15.2 God prunes, literally 'purifies' (καθαίρει) the fruitful vine branch; in 13.10 he who has been baptized is entirely clean (καθαρός), but needs periodical feet-washing, i.e. the Eucharist, to remove post-baptismal sins. Further confirmation, if any were needed, of the eucharistic reference of the miracle at Cana is to be found in the statement that in working this first sign Jesus 'manifested his glory' (verse 11). This only has point if the production of wine anticipates the gift of eucharistic wine which corresponds to Christ's giving of his blood on the cross in his 'glorification'.[2]

The Bread of Life, 6.1-14, 26-71

If the evangelist had the Eucharist in mind in writing his account of the feeding of the multitude, he was following an already existing tradition which is reflected in the eucharistic character of the feeding of the four thousand in Mark, where (8.6) as in John 6.11, 23, εὐχαριστήσας replaces the εὐλόγησε of the narrative of the five thousand in Mark 6.41. That the evangelist regarded the miracle as eucharistic seems to be indicated by the

---

[1] M. Goguel, L'église primitive, 1948, p. 370; O. Cullmann, op. cit., pp. 67-72.

[2] O. Cullmann, op. cit., pp. 75 f suggests that the words 'the temple of his body' in 2.21, while (in his view) meaning primarily, in accord with the Pauline doctrine, the Church as the body of Christ (so R. H. Strachan, The Fourth Gospel, 3rd edn., 1941, p. 127; cf. G. H. C. Macgregor, The Gospel of John, 1936 (=1928), pp. 62 f), also contain an allusion to the presence of the body of Christ in the eucharistic bread, and that they thus form a parallel to the eucharistic blood in the immediately preceding Cana narrative. This view is improbable, because the interpretation of 'the temple of his body' upon which it depends is itself untenable for the reason that the object of 'destroy' and of 'I will raise it up' in verse 19 must be one and the same. Cf. R. Bultmann, op. cit., Ergänzungsheft, 1950, p. 19 (n. to p. 90).

mention of the proximity of the Passover (verse 4), because the narrative of the foot-washing in chapter thirteen, which is an allegory of the Eucharist, is introduced by the statement that the supper took place before the feast of the Passover.

The rest of the sixth chapter from verse 26 onwards, after the discovery of Jesus at Capernaum, consists of the discourse on the bread of life (verses 26-59), which takes the form of a dispute with the Jews in the synagogue, an explanation of the difficult teaching for the benefit of doubting disciples (verses 60-65), and the contrast between the confession of Peter and the treachery of Judas (verses 66-71). If the writer had the Eucharist in mind in describing the miracle, he must have had it in mind in composing the *whole* of the discourse and the following section which is closely connected with it. The allusions to the treachery of Judas in verses 64 and 70 f, firstly veiled and then direct, recall corresponding references in the eucharistic framework of the thirteenth chapter (verses 10 f, 21-30).

A number of scholars, however, have not held this view, but have seen in the mention of 'flesh' in verse 51*b* the introduction of a fresh thought, and have regarded verses 51*b*-58 as a redactional addition in the interests of eucharistic doctrine. In the preceding discourse, which alone is original, the words of Jesus about himself as the bread of life refer to his teaching, and to obtain eternal life by eating the bread is to do so by believing in him. So F. Spitta,[1] who detected a new note already in verse 51*a*, 'I am the living bread', which, as distinct from 'the bread of life', denoted the (living) flesh of Christ; saw at this point an abrupt transition from the earthly mission of Jesus to the Eucharist; and, viewing verses 51-58 as a eucharistic doublet of the preceding discourse, pointed to the use of the manna in both passages as the ineffective counterpart of the heavenly bread (verses 31 f, 49 f, 58). R. Bultmann, in his commentary, sees revelation through the Word as the leading motive in the Fourth Gospel, and, in accord with his theory of its negative attitude to sacraments,

---

[1] *Zur Geschichte und Litteratur des Urchristentums*, i, 1893, pp. 216-221.

Johannine Eucharistic Doctrine

pronounces verses 51b-58 to be a later eucharistic addition.[1] This dislocation of the discourse is due to a misunderstanding, for it is characteristic of the method of this Gospel that the bread of life should be both the Jesus of history who reveals the truth about God in words which are spirit and life, and the Christ who is present in the eucharistic bread which is his flesh.[2]

We turn firstly to the eucharistic traits of the discourse as far as verse 51a, for even those who deny the unity of the whole pericope concede the eucharistic nature of the remainder, verses 51b-58.

The eschatological outlook and joyful awaiting of the Messianic Kingdom are, as we have seen earlier, an inherent element of the Lord's Supper in the New Testament. This is not absent from the Fourth Gospel, although, as with so much else, it is transposed into another key. It is represented by the thrice repeated promise of the Lord, 'I will raise him up at the last day' (6.39, 40, 44).[3]

Paul alludes to the manna, the 'supernatural food' which the fathers enjoyed in the wilderness, as the type of the bread of the Eucharist (1 Cor. 10.3). In John 6.31 the Jews recall the manna, the 'bread from heaven' (Ex. 16.4; Ps. 78.24; Wisdom 16.20), and expect Jesus to prove himself by a repetition of the miracle. Jesus replies that he is the true bread from heaven which, unlike the manna, provides life. The manna is not, as with Paul, the counterpart to the eucharistic bread, but a pointer, ineffective in itself, to this bread. This is made explicit in the second mention of the manna. 'Your fathers ate the manna in the wilderness, and died. This is the bread which comes down from heaven, that a man may eat of it and not die' (verses 49 f; cf. 58). This use of the

---

[1] Op. cit., pp. 161 f; so also, among others, H. Odeberg, *The Fourth Gospel*, 1929; J. Jeremias, op. cit., p. 59; and E. Schweizer, *Ego Eimi*, 1939, pp. 155 f, who, with J. E. Carpenter, *The Johannine Writings*, 1927, p. 428, n. 2, points out differences of phraseology in these verses. Professor Filson has kindly pointed out that E. Ruckstuhl (*Die literarische Einheit des Johannesevangeliums*, 1951, pp. 220-271) opposes the point of view as stated by Jeremias.

[2] See O. Cullmann, op. cit., pp. 89-99 for an incisive defence of the unity of the discourse; cf. also E. C. Hoskyns, op. cit., p. 305.

[3] It occurs again in verse 54, where alone, according to Bultmann (op. cit., p.162), it is natural, because only in verses 51b-58 is there anything about the life-giving properties of the eucharistic elements, its presence in the other three places being the work of the redactor.

manna in this context in a way similar to but not identical with that of Paul helps to stamp the passage as eucharistic. It is also possible that the writer was influenced by the notion, as expressed by Philo, that the manna was a type of the divine Logos as the heavenly food of the soul.[1]

The introduction of the manna also corresponds to that looking forward to the Messianic banquet which is an integral part of the Lord's Supper. In the Syriac Apocalypse of Baruch it is said of the Messianic age that 'the treasury of manna shall again descend from on high' (2 *Baruch* 29.8), and it was believed that the Messiah would bring down the manna as Moses did.[2]

The final verses 51*b*-58, which contain the most unmistakable eucharistic allusions, are part and parcel of the whole discourse on the bread of life, to which it is intended to provide a climax. The Jews are confronted in the most outspoken language with the belief and the rite which they find abhorrent, and wavering Christians are challenged with the claim that these are indispensable. The bread which Jesus gives now turns out to be his flesh. The Jews misunderstand, thinking that the man they see before them is meant, whereas it is the Christ who is present in the Eucharist. The drinking of the blood would be a still more repugnant idea to them. But it is needful for real life to eat the flesh and drink the blood of the Son of Man, 'for my flesh is real food, and my blood is real drink'. The necessity of eating the flesh of the Son of Man is driven home uncompromisingly by the transition to the word 'munch' ($\tau\rho\omega\gamma\epsilon\iota\nu$) for 'eat' in verses 54, 56-58. It is a real eating that is meant. The Christ at the Eucharist is as real as was his human body.

The use of the term 'flesh' is connected with the anti-docetic purpose of the Gospel and with the identity of the incarnate Christ with the Christ of the Eucharist. Is it, however, the case that for his own purposes the evangelist has deliberately substituted 'flesh' for the 'body' of the traditional word of institution,

[1] Cf. R. Bultmann, op. cit., p. 169, n. 5.
[2] Strack-Billerbeck, *Kommentar zum Neuen Testament aus Talmud und Midrasch*, ii, 1924, p. 481; H. Odeberg, op. cit., pp. 242 f; E. C. Hoskyns, op. cit., pp. 293 f.

Johannine Eucharistic Doctrine

'This is my body'? Thus Hoskyns writes: 'The substitution of *Flesh* for *Body* is the natural corollary to i. 14',[1] and Carpenter remarks: ' "Body" became "flesh" because the Church was endangered by the denial that Jesus had come in the flesh'; 'body' might denote something unsubstantial and exempt from suffering.[2] But it is possible that the evangelist did not substitute one term for another, but gave the preference, as more suitable to his purpose, to a branch of the tradition of the eucharistic words of Jesus in which the elements were *flesh* and blood.[3]

The next section (from verse 60) turns from the Jews whose opposition has been met in the discussion in the synagogue, to disciples, representing Christians of a later day, who found what Jesus had been saying about eating his flesh 'a hard saying' and difficult to believe. The retort of Jesus is, 'What then if you were to see the Son of Man ascending where he was before? It is the Spirit that gives life, the flesh is of no avail; the words which I have spoken to you are spirit and life' (verses 62 f). The contradiction of what has gone before in the statement about the ineffectiveness of the flesh is only apparent, for what imparts their life-giving efficacy to the eucharistic elements is the Spirit released by the ascension. The vitally important factor in the incarnation was that it was the *Logos* that was incarnate. The signs Jesus wrought he wrought not as flesh but as Logos; here too it was equally true that the flesh in itself availed nothing. The flesh that was effective in the incarnation was *living* flesh, vivified by the Spirit. The same is true of the eucharistic flesh, for the Eucharist is 'the concretion of the Christ incarnate'.[4] The relevance of the saying, 'the words which I have spoken to you are spirit and life' is not at first evident. But the words which are spirit and life, meaning primarily but not exclusively the foregoing discourse

---

[1] Op. cit., p. 297.   [2] Op. cit., p. 434.
[3] See above, p. 49, n. 2. Perhaps a conscious reversion to the other tradition is to be recognized in the translation of σάρξ in verses 51-58 and 63 by the word for 'body' in the Old Syriac and the Peshitta; note also D's addition to verse 56 (partly paralleled in two Old Latin manuscripts), which includes the words, 'if you do not receive the *body* of the Son of Man'.
[4] E. C. Hoskyns, op. cit., p. 305.

on the bread of life, are so intimately associated with the Eucharist that the evangelist sees no contrast between eucharistic discourse and the Eucharist itself.[1] The author's answer, then, to misunderstandings of the sacrament is that the eating and drinking of flesh and blood, while real, is not physical, but spiritual, and corresponds to the physical partaking of the bread and wine.

This emphasis on the spiritual character of the rite is doubtless an attack on magical views derived from the mystery cults. The same polemic accounts for the stress laid on the necessity of belief. This is evident both in the first section of the discourse (verses 29, 35, 36, 40, 47), and in the use of the Jews and the withdrawing disciples as types of unbelief (cf. verse 64) in contrast with Peter and the loyal disciples who believe (verse 69), while Judas is the glaring example of the perdition to which unbelief leads.

The Foot-Washing, 13.1-20

The foot-washing takes the place of the institution of the Eucharist at the Last Supper. The reply of Jesus to Peter's objection to receiving this lowly service at the hands of his Master, 'If I do not wash you, you have no part with me', points to the necessity of the Eucharist for the enjoyment of union with Christ. When Peter then desires to have his hands and head washed as well as his feet, the answer of Jesus, 'He who has bathed has no need to wash, except his feet, but is wholly clean', means that baptism washes away sin and cannot be repeated, but that from time to time purification from post-baptismal sins in the Eucharist is necessary.

The foot-washing is an allegory of the Eucharist, and the Johannine parallel to the command of Jesus that it is to be repeated in his memory is to be found partly in the words, 'If I then, the Lord and Master, have washed your feet, you also ought to wash one another's feet. For I have given you an example, that you also should do as I have done to you.' It is a command not

---

[1] Cf. E. C. Hoskyns, op. cit., pp. 305 f, who refers to 'interpenetration of Word and Sacrament'.

Johannine Eucharistic Doctrine

to neglect the fellowship of the Church at its common meal, for here lies the way to communion with Christ himself. This emphasis on the ethical aspect of the Eucharist is repeated in the new commandment of love (verses 34 f), which is but a different expression of the injunction that the disciples follow his example in washing one another's feet, and in its turn corresponds partly to the command to repeat the Eucharist and partly to the new covenant in Paul and Luke.[1]

The Farewell Discourses, 13.31-17.26

The traitor has just made his dramatic exit, 'and it was night'. But Jesus rejoices, for his glorification through death, which will bring him back to the Father, is about to commence.

In the promise of the Lord, 'I will come again' (14.3, 18, 28) is reflected the eager expectation cherished by the Church of his return in glory at the Parousia and the conviction that this was anticipated in his gracious presence at the breaking of bread. Of course, in the Fourth Gospel the hope of the Lord's return is bound up with the sending of the Paraclete; but we may say that the early eucharistic petition *marana tha*, 'Our Lord, come' finds its place in this eucharistic framework of the farewell discourses in the form of Christ's response, so to speak, to the appeal of his friends that he should return to them.

But it is in the fifteenth chapter that the eucharistic thought is clearest. Here the vine represents the eucharistic wine, as it does in the *Didache* 9.2, 'the holy vine of thy servant David'. We are reminded, too, of the word of Jesus at the Last Supper that he would not again drink of the fruit of the vine until the reunion

---

[1] For this sacramental interpretation see M. Goguel, *L'eucharistie des origines à Justin Martyr*, 1910, p. 195; *L'église primitive*, 1948, p. 369; O. Cullmann, op. cit., pp. 102-106. Bultmann, as elsewhere, sees no sacramental reference here, and calls 'grotesque' the idea that the foot-washing represents the Eucharist (op. cit., p.3 57, n. 5). Rejecting εἰ μὴ τοὺς πόδας (lacking in Codex Sinaiticus and some Latin authorities) in verse 10 as an interpolation, Bultmann explains the passage as meaning that he who accepts the service of Christ, i.e. believes his word, is clean (verse 10; cf. 15.3), and needs no further means of salvation. M. J. Lagrange, *Évangile selon saint Jean*, 8th edn., 1948, pp. 348 f sees in the story purely a lesson in humility and condescension.

in the Kingdom of God (Mark 14.25; Luke 22.18). Nothing is said of the bread because that occupies the central position in the eucharistic discourse in the sixth chapter. The fifteenth chapter is, in fact, a very close counterpart to the sixth. To 15.1, '*I am* the *true vine*, and *my Father* is the vinedresser' correspond 6.35, 'I am the bread of life' and 6.32, '*My Father* gives you the *true bread* from heaven'. The Father both supplies the bread and tends the vine. In both chapters communion with Christ is described as a mutual abiding of the believer in Christ and of Christ in the believer. The metaphors differ, but only externally. In 6.56 f he who eats the flesh and drinks the blood of Christ receives his divine life; in 15.4 f the disciples are like the branches of a vine which are wholly dependent for their existence on the trunk, from which they drink in the life-giving sap. Again, the apostasy of the Jews, and of Judas and of unbelievers among the disciples in chapter six is balanced by the useless branches which are cut off and burned.

The contacts with chapter thirteen are equally striking. In 13.10 f he who has been baptized is clean, but needs the periodical purification of the Eucharist; all the disciples, however, were not clean, for among them was the traitor. In 15.2 f the disciples are clean, but there are unproductive branches which are removed. The fruitful branches God prunes (literally 'cleanses', καθαίρει) to increase their yield. The words, 'A servant is not greater than his master' (13.16) are recalled (in 15.20), as is also the commandment to love one another (13.34; 15.12, 17).

Chapter seventeen, the climax of the whole section, comprises the high-priestly prayer of Jesus, which replaces the eucharistic actions reported by the other Gospels and by Paul, for the Eucharist, in the view of the evangelist, could only take place after Christ's death. Although in a sense the evangelist portrays Jesus as presiding at the prototype of the Church's Eucharist, the eucharistic prayer is such as only Jesus could have uttered, for he is consecrating himself (17.19) as the source of the flesh and blood which are to be the food of the future Eucharist. Yet the prayer is clothed in language which must have been familiar to the evan-

Johannine Eucharistic Doctrine

gelist from the practice of his day, and which bears certain resemblances to the phraseology of the *Didache*. Among these resemblances may be noted: 'Holy Father', 17.11; *Didache* 10.2; protection from evil, 17.11, 15; *Didache* 10.5; the perfecting of the Church in love, 17.23; *Didache* 10.5. Again, the impassioned prayer 'that they may be one' (17.11, 21, 23) is paralleled in the *Didache* by the prayer for the gathering of the Church from the four winds into the Kingdom (10.5), and by the similar prayer which compares the far-flung Church which is to be so gathered with the loaf which was scattered in the sowing 'and being gathered together became one' (9.4). This idea of the unity of the Church, common to the Fourth Gospel and the *Didache*, is shared also by Paul, who sees the oneness of the Church in its partaking of one loaf (1 Cor. 10.17).

The Spear-thrust, 19.34

'But one of the soldiers pierced his side with a spear, and immediately there came out blood and water.' The main reason for the inclusion of this incident is not anti-docetic, to show that Jesus really died upon the cross, but to express the belief that the two sacraments were founded on, or flowed from the death of Christ. This is because both baptism and the Eucharist derive their efficacy from the operation of the Spirit, and the Spirit is given only after the death of Christ. The passage in 1 John 5.6-8, which is dependent on this narrative, explicitly couples the witness of the Spirit with that of the water and the blood. But its relevance here is its special emphasis on the blood, i.e. on the actual death of Christ and on the Eucharist as its liturgical counterpart. 'This is he who came by water and blood, Jesus Christ, not with the water only but with the water and the blood.' The same emphasis on the blood, i.e. on the Eucharist, is present also in John 19.34. Not only is the blood mentioned first, but after the reiteration of the trustworthiness of the eye-witness there follows a quotation from the ritual law of the paschal victim (Ex. 12.46; Num. 9.12), 'A bone of him shall not be broken'. There are thus present in deliberate juxtaposition the two ideas of the genesis of the Eucharist and the death of the paschal victim. At the beginning of the Gospel John the Baptist had recognized in Jesus the Lamb of God (1.29, 36), the true (paschal) lamb.[1] At the end of the story Christ the true paschal lamb dies and is henceforth remembered and feasted upon at the Eucharist.

[1] For the equation of τοῦ θεοῦ and ἀληθινός see Bultmann, op. cit., p. 67 n. The clearest example is 6.32 f, where 'the true bread' = 'the bread of God'.

CONCLUSION

It lies beyond the province of this book to draw out the implications of the results of this study of the Lord's Supper in the New Testament for contemporary eucharistic practice. But among these results the following stand out as of special relevance.

(1) The problem of the 'dominical institution' of the Eucharist cannot be handled in isolation from the question whether Jesus 'founded' the Church.

(2) The Church and its Eucharist are the historical counterparts of what Jesus envisaged—a new Israel, the Messianic community, and its Passover centred upon his own death.

(3) The earliest churches, in remembering the death of Christ, at the same time rejoiced in his living, risen presence at the breaking of bread.

(4) The 'real presence' was therefore not found in the eucharistic elements, whose role rather was to recall the sacrificial death of Christ as *event*.

(5) The joy of knowing the presence of Christ at the Eucharist was a foretaste of the final reunion in the Kingdom of God.

INDEX OF REFERENCES

OLD TESTAMENT

Bible Ref.	Page	Bible Ref.	Page
Genesis		**Numbers**	
17.10	33	20.7 ff	67
49.11	52	21.16	67
		Deuteronomy	
Exodus		16.3	35, 53
1.14	46	17.13	18
12	50	21.22 f	20
12.5	51, n. 1	32.14	52
12.8	20, n. 4	**Psalms**	
12.14	35	78.24	81
12.26 f	36, 46	105.39	66
12.39	46	113, 114	46
12.46	77, 87	114-118, 115-118	21
13.3, 9	36	**Isaiah**	
13.8	36, 46	41.27	47
13.21 f	66	53.12	32
14.21 f	66	**Jeremiah**	
16.4	66, 81	16.7	56
16.14-18	66	31.31 ff	30, n. 6, 33, 34, n. 2
17.6	66		
24.8	31	**Lamentations**	
Leviticus		4.4	56
16	51	**Daniel**	
17.10-12	30, n. 1	7	10 f
23.10 f, 15	23, n.	7.27	11
		Malachi	
Numbers		3.16 f	11, n. 3
9.12	77, 87		

APOCRYPHA AND PSEUDEPIGRAPHA

Bible Ref.	Page	Bible Ref.	Page
Wisdom of Solomon		**Jubilees**	
16.20	81	49.1, 12	20, n. 4
19.7	66	49.6, 9	21
2 Baruch		**Zadokite Work**	
29.8	82	9.28	30, n. 6
1 Enoch			
62.14	48		

Index of References

NEW TESTAMENT

Bible Ref.	Page	Bible Ref.	Page
Matthew		**Mark**	
3.7, 11	10	14.34 f	75
8.11	48	14.62	11, n. 1
10.7	10, n.	15.21, 25, 46	19
12.28	10, n.		
16.16-18	12, n. 1		
19.28	11	**Luke**	
22.1 ff	48	3.7, 16	10
26.1-5	17	10.9, 11	10, n.
26.20	20	11.20	10, n.
26.21, 30	21	12.32	11
26.23	20	13.29	48
26.25	22	22.14	20
26.26	21, n. 1	22.15	16, 20, n. 2, 38, 40, 45, 47
26.26-29	24	22.15-18	40, 42, 47-49
		22.15-19a	15, n. 3, 40, 42, 43, 58
Mark			
1.15	10	22.15-20	24, 37-44
6.41	79	22.16	11, 38, 40, 41, 42, 45
8.6	79		
8.29, 31	10	22.17	15, n. 3, 38, 39, n. 1, 40, 45
8.38	11, n. 1, 75		
9.1	11, n. 1	22.17 f	41
10.45	50	22.18	11, 37, 38, 39, n. 1, 40, 41, 42, 45, 86
13.26	11, n. 1		
14.1 f	17		
14.12, 14, 16	20, n. 2		
14.17, 30	20, n. 3	22.19	29, n. 2, 46, 55
14.18	20, 21, n. 1	22.19a	38, 40
14.20	20	22.19a-20	43
14.22	17, 21, n. 1, 28 f, 46, 49-54	22.19b-20	38, 39, 40
		22.19-20	43, 44
14.22-24	43	22.20	46
14.22-25	24	22.29 f	11
14.23	46	22.30	11, 48
14.24	24, n. 1, 29-34, 46, 49-54	22.38	18
		22.43	75
14.25	11, 24, n. 1, 28, 32, 37, 41, 45, 47-49, 60, 86	23.26	19
		24.30, 35	56
		24.30-35	61
14.26	18, 21, 47	24.36-43	61, 63
14.32, 43, 47, 48	18	24.44-49	62, n. 2

Index of References

Bible Ref.	Page	Bible Ref.	Page
John		John	
1.14	77, 83	13.30, 26-30, 29	22
1.29, 36	77, 88	13.21-30	80
1.32 f, 51	75	13.23, 28	20, 22
2.1-11	78 f	13.30	20, n. 3
2.6	79	13.31-17, 26	85-87
2.11	78, 79	13.34 f	85
2.19, 21	79, n. 2	14.3, 18, 28	85
3.1 ff, 13	75	14.21, 23	61, n. 3
4.1 ff	75	15.1, 2 f, 4 f, 12, 17, 20	86
6.1-14, 26-71	79-84	15.2	79
6.4, 26-59, 31 f, 60-65, 66-71, 70 f	80	15.3	85, n.
		17.11, 15, 21, 23	87
6.11, 23	79	17.19	86
6.29, 36, 47, 69	84	18.1, 28	22
6.31, 39, 44, 49 f	81	19.14	22
6.32, 56 f	86	19.31, 31-37, 42	22, n. 3
6.32 f	88, n.	19.34	75, 87 f
6.35	84, 86	19.36	77
6.40	81, 84	20.17	75
6.49 f	80, 81	20.31	77
6.51-56	49, n. 2	21.9 ff	61
6.51-58	80-83	21.15-17	61, n. 3
6.54	81, n. 3, 82	Acts	
6.56	83, n. 3	1.4	61, 62
6.56-58	82	1.4 f	62, n. 2
6.60, 62 f	83	2.42	56, 57
6.60-66	76	2.42-47	57
6.62	75	2.46	56, 57, 61
6.63	49, n. 2, 83, n. 3	10.41	54, 61, 62
6.64	80, 84	10.42 f	62, n. 2
7.6, 8, 30	78	20.7, 11	56
7.39	77	20.7-11	57
8.20	78	27.35	56, n. 1
12.23	78	Romans	
12.27	75	3.25	69
13-17	61, n. 3	5.9	69
13.1	22, 78	7.4	73
13.1-20	75, 84 f	8.10, 17	69
13.10	79, 85 n.	8.38	68, n. 3
13.10 f	80, 86	9.4	31
13.12, 25	20	11.27	31
13.16, 34	86		

Index of References

Bible Ref.	Page
1 Corinthians	
1.24, 30	67
2.8	68, n. 3
5.2, 13	64
5.6	64, n.
5.6-8	64 f
5.7	49
7.10, 25	28
9.14	28
10.1-22	64, 65-70
10.3	81
10.14, 22	67
10.14-21	65
10.16	15, n. 3, 38, 46, 56, 69, 70
10.16 f	27
10.17	70, 87
10.18, 19	68
10.21	15, n. 3, 38, 68
11	57
11.17-22	64
11.18-34	70-73
11.20	60
11.22	60, 71, 73
11.23	17, 20, n. 3, 25, 28, 71
11.23-25	24, 27, n. 1, 43 f
11.23-26	64, 71
11.24	28 f, 34-36, 46, 55
11.25	26, n. 13, 29-34, 34-36, 46, 59, 69
11.26	26, n. 13, 37, 53, 55, n. 1, 60
11.27	63, 72, n. 3, 73
11.27-29	70
11.27-30	71
11.27-34	64, 67
11.29, 32	73
11.34	60, 71
12.12 f, 13, 27	69
15.3-5	25
15.20	65
16.22	60

Bible Ref.	Page
2 Corinthians	
3.6	33
3.6 ff	31
5.17	69
Galatians	
1.12	25
2.20	69
3.15 ff	31
3.27	69
4.9	68, n. 3
4.24 ff	31
5.9	64, n.
Ephesians	
2.12	31
6.11 f	68, n. 3
Philippians	
3.10	70
Colossians	
1.7	25, n. 2, 28, n. 2
1.15-17	67
1.27	69
2.8	68, n. 3
1 Thessalonians	
4.15	28
Hebrews	
6.6	72, n. 3
10.29	72, n. 3
1 Peter	
1.19	49, 65, n. 2
1 John	
4.1-3	76
5.6-8	87
2 John	
7	76
Jude	
12	60, n. 2

93

Index of References

Bible Ref.	Page	Bible Ref.	Page
Revelation		Revelation	
3.20	61, 62	14.20	52
5.6	49, 65, n. 2	19.9	48, n. 4

CHRISTIAN WRITINGS

Acts of John		Didache	
85 f	58, n. 2	9.4	87
109 f	58, n. 2	10.1–5	38
Acts of Peter		10.2, 5	87
5	58, n. 2	10.6	38, 60
Didache		14	38
9	38	Epistle of the Apostles	
9.2	85	15	54, n. 2

JEWISH WRITINGS

Targum Onkelos:		Babylonian Talmud:	
Numbers 21.19	67	Berakoth 46a, 47a	56, n. 2
		Shabbath 151a	19, n. 3
Mishnah:		Jerusalem Talmud:	
Berakoth 6.1	45, n. 2	Pesahim 10.1	20, n. 5
Betzah 5.2	18, n. 3	Mekhilta, Exodus 12.42	47, n. 2
Pesahim 5.10	20, n. 4		
10.1	21, n. 2	Tosephta:	
10.2	15, n. 3, 45, n. 2	Shabbath 17.13	19, n. 3
10.3	20, n. 6	Sukkah 3.11	67, n. 2
10.4, 5	46, n.	Exodus Rabbah 15.1	47, n. 3
Sanhedrin 4.1	18, n. 4	18.11	47, n. 1
Zebahim 5.8	20, n. 4	18.12	48, n. 1

INDEX OF AUTHORS

Barth, M., 23, n. 1, 53, 54
Bate, H. N., 40, n. 1
Beare, F. W., 51, n. 2
Behm, J., 30, n. 6, 31, 33, 42, n. 6, 45, n. 1
Benoit, P., 35
Box, G. H., 14, n.
Bultmann, R., 23, n., 26, 32, n. 2, 38, n. 2, 40, n. 1, 60, n. 1, 74, 79, n. 2, 80, 81, n. 3, 82, n. 1, 85, n., 88, n.

Carpenter, J. E., 81, n. 1, 83
Cirlot, F. L., 15, n. 4, 26
Coates, J. R., 12, n. 1
Cullmann, O., 28, 61, 62, n. 1, 63 77, n. 1, 79, n. 2, 81, n. 2, 85, n'

Dalman, G., 17, n. 1, 18, n. 1, 19, n. 2, 20, n. 1, 23, n. 1, 29, n. 1, 33, 39, n. 2, 45, n. 1, 48, 49, n. 2, 50, n. 2, 53, n. 2, 56, n. 2
Davies, W. D., 27, 28, n. 3, 34, 36
Dibelius, M., 26, 30, n. 4, 34, n. 1
Dix, G., 15, n. 4
Dodd, C. H., 11, n. 3

Epiphanius, 55, n. 2
Etheridge, J. W., 67, n. 1

Finkelstein, L., 23, n.
Flew, R. N., 29, n. 4, 30, n. 6

Gaugler, E., 15, 23, n. 1, 24, n. 2, 26, 33, 39, n. 3, 53
Gavin, F., 15, n. 1
Gloege, G., 12, n. 1
Goetz, K. G., 49, n. 2
Goguel, M., 23, n. 1, 26, 41, 42, n. 6, 61, n. 2, 69, n. 1, 72, n. 2, 77, n. 2, 79, n. 1, 85, n.
Goodspeed, E. J., 66, n. 3
Gray, G. B., 50, n. 2, 51, n. 1
Green, A. A., 48, n. 2, 53, n. 2

Héring, J., 26, 67, 71, n., 72, n. 2
Hippolytus, 57
Holtzmann, H. J., 41, n. 4
Hoskyns, E. C., 76, n. 2, 81, n. 2, 82, n. 2, 83, 84, n.

Ignatius, 49, n. 2, 72, 76

James, M. R., 54, n. 2
Jeremias, J., 7, 15, 16, n. 2, 17, n. 1, 18, 19, 21, n. 3, 22, 23, n. 1, 24, n. 1, n. 2, 25, n. 3, 27, n. 1, 33, 34, n. 2, 35, n. 1, 37, n., 38, 39, n. 2, 42, n. 1, n. 3, 44, n. 1, 45, n. 1, 49, n. 2, 50, n. 1, n. 3, 53, n. 2, 55, n. 1, 56, 59, n. 1, 74, n. 2, 81, n. 1

Kennett, R. H., 49, n. 3
Kilpatrick, G. D., 39, n. 2
Kittel, G., 12, n. 1, 30, n. 6, 31, n. 2, 33, n. 5, 42, n. 6, 45, n. 1, 60, n. 1
Klausner, J., 30, n. 2
Knox, W. L., 74, n. 2
Kümmel, W. G., 26, 72, n. 3

Lagrange, M. J., 85, n.
Leenhardt, F. J., 13, n., 23, n. 1, 25, n. 4, 30, 31, 32, 42, n. 2, 69, n. 2, 72, n. 3
Lietzmann, H., 15, 23, n. 1, 24, n. 2, 25, 26, 35, 36, 40, 57, 58, 60, 61, 68, n. 1, 72, n. 1, n. 2, n. 3
Loewe, H., 30
Lohmeyer, E., 23, n. 1, 26, 27, n. 2, 39, n. 3, 58, n. 1, 74
Loisy, A., 25, n. 1, 41, n. 2

Macdonald, A. B., 26, n. 1
Macgregor, G. H. C., 15, n. 1, 42, n. 5, 79, n. 2
Manson, T. W., 11, n. 1
Moffatt, J., 66, n. 3, 72

Index of Authors

Montefiore, C. G., 30
Moore, G. F., 48, n. 2

Odeberg, H., 81, n. 1, 82, n. 2
Oesterley, W. O. E., 15, n. 1, n. 2
Otto, R., 15, n. 4
Oulton, J. E. L., 15, n. 4

Philo, 67, 82
Preiss, T., 16, 26

Ruckstuhl, E., 81, n. 1

Sarapion, 57
Schlatter, A., 59, n. 1
Schmidt, K. L., 12, 40, n. 1, 58, n. 1
Schoeps, H. J., 55, n. 2, 58, n. 2, 62, n. 1
Schweitzer, A., 26, 48, n. 4, 49

Schweizer, E., 41, n. 4, 42, n. 4, 54, n. 2, 81, n. 1
Scott, C. A. A., 72, n. 3
Selwyn, E. G., 51, n. 2
Spitta, F., 14, n., 57, 58, n. 2, 61, n. 2, 80
Stauffer, E., 23, n. 1
Strachan, R. H., 79, n. 2
Strack-Billerbeck, 16, n. 1, 17, n. 1, 21, n. 4, 23, n., 26, n. 11, 45, n. 1, 66, n. 1, n. 2, 68, n. 2, 82, n. 2

Taylor, V., 11, 30, n. 3, 54, n. 2

van Unnik, W. C., 55, n. 1

Weiss, J., 26, 29, 65, n. 1, 72, n. 1, n. 2

Zahn, T., 55, n. 2

www.ingramcontent.com/pod-product-compliance
Lightning Source LLC
Chambersburg PA
CBHW051407290426
44108CB00015B/2193